IBADAH CREATIONS

Ramadan Planner 2026

Copyright ©2026

What's Inside This Ramadan Planner

This planner is designed to help you make the most of your Ramadan — spiritually, mentally, and emotionally. Inside, you will find:

📖 **Qur'an Tracker**

Track your daily Qur'an reading and stay consistent throughout the month.

🌙 **Fast Tracker**

Mark each fast and reflect on your discipline and dedication.

🕌 **Taraweeh Tracker**

Keep a record of your Taraweeh prayers and motivate yourself to stay regular.

🤲 **Ramadan Duas**

A special collection of powerful duas for forgiveness, guidance, and gratitude.

📅 **Daily Planner Pages**

Plan your day, set goals, and reflect on your actions and feelings.

✨ **Asma-ul-Husna (99 Names of Allah)**

Meanings and reflections on each of Allah's beautiful names to help you build a deeper connection with Him.

💡 **30 Days Ramadan Challenge**

Complete the recitation of the whole quran and also memorise surahs.

Table for Prayer Rakat

Preface: The Journey of the Heart

Welcome to your 2026 Ramadan companion.

Every year, we approach Ramadan with a list of goals: to finish the Quran, to pray every Taraweeh, and to perfect our fasts. But often, in the busyness of the schedule, we forget the essence of the One for whom we are doing it all.

This year's edition was born out of a desire to move beyond the "checklist" and into a state of Ma'rifah——deep, intimate knowledge of Allah (SWT). To know Him is to love Him; and to love Him is to find ease in every prostration and sweetness in every hour of hunger.

Why the Names of Allah?

By integrating the Asma-ul-Husna (The Most Beautiful Names) into your daily planning, this book seeks to transform your worship from a physical act into a spiritual dialogue.

When you track your habits, you do so under the gaze of Al-Basir (The All-Seeing).

When you seek forgiveness, you turn to Al-Ghaffar (The Repeatedly Forgiving).

When you feel overwhelmed by your goals, you lean on Al-Wakeel (The Best Disposer of Affairs).

How to Journey with this Planner

This planner is not a judge; it is a witness. If you miss a goal, do not be discouraged. Simply return to the pages, find a Name of Allah that brings you comfort, and start again. The goal of this month is not perfection——it is sincerity.

As we navigate the 30 days of 2026, let this book be a quiet space for your reflections, a mirror for your growth, and a bridge to the Divine.

With prayers for your success and illumination,

The Creator of the 2026 Ramadan Planner

Copyright ©2026

Acknowledgement

The creation of this 2026 Ramadan Planner has been a journey of faith, and it would not have been possible without the support, inspiration, and guidance of many hands and hearts.

To The Most High

First and foremost, all praise and thanks belong to Allah (SWT), Al-Fattah (The Opener), who opened the doors of inspiration and provided the strength to bring this vision to life for another year. This work is a humble effort to serve His Ummah, and any benefit found within these pages is through His grace alone.

To My Family and Friends

To my family, thank you for your patience and for providing the quiet space I needed to curate these pages. Your encouragement during the long nights of designing and writing was the fuel that kept this project moving forward.

To the Scholars and Mentors

I am deeply indebted to the teachers and scholars whose insights into the Asma-ul-Husna (The Names of Allah) provided the spiritual framework for this year's upgrade.

To You, the User

Finally, to you—the one holding this planner. Thank you for choosing this guide to be a part of your most sacred month. Your commitment to spiritual growth is what gives this project meaning. May this planner serve you well, and I humbly ask that you remember me and my family in your sincere Duas during the hours of Iftar and Tahajjud.

Dedication

This edition is dedicated to those seeking to find their way back to Allah. May His Names guide you home.

Ibadah Creations

The Essence of Ramadan: A Month of Mercy

To make this page more engaging for your planner, we can structure it with inspiring headings, a cleaner flow, and a focus on the spiritual "why" behind the fast. This transforms it from a simple definition into a motivational "Call to Action" for the user.

Here is a refined version of your Ramadan Info page:

The Essence of Ramadan: A Month of Mercy

"...But to fast is best for you, if you only knew." — Surat Al-Baqarah 2:184

Ramadan is the ninth and most sacred month of the Islamic calendar—a divine appointment between the Creator and the created. It marks the period when the Holy Quran was first sent down as a guiding light for humanity, directing our hearts toward everything beneficial in this world and the next.

Why We Fast (Sawm)

Fasting is more than the physical act of abstaining from food and drink from dawn until sunset. It is a holistic purification of the soul. By practicing restraint, we learn to:

- **Master the Self:** Gain control over worldly desires and impulses.

- **Deepen Taqwa:** Cultivate a constant awareness of Allah (SWT).

- **Empathize:** Feel the hunger of the less fortunate, sparking a drive for social justice and charity.

The Essence of Ramadan: A Month of Mercy

The Night Prayer: Standing in Taraweeh, seeking stillness in the late hours.

The Final Revelation: Not just reading the Quran, but reflecting on its wisdom and applying it to our lives.

Radical Generosity: Giving Sadaqah and providing meals (Iftar) for those in need.

Prophetic Character: Following the Sunnah of Prophet Muhammad (ﷺ) through refined manners, patience, and kindness toward family and community.

Your Journey Begins

As you open these pages, remember that Ramadan is a gift—a chance to hit the "reset" button on your soul. Every moment of restraint, every verse recited, and every act of kindness is a noble step beloved by Allah (SWT).

Make this month count. Not just in the hunger of your stomach, but in the awakening of your heart.

Key Reminders for the Month:

Intentionality (Niyyah): Start every day by renewing your intention for the sake of Allah. Consistency: Allah loves deeds that are consistent, even if they are small. Reflection: Use the quiet moments of your fast to listen to what your soul truly needs.

Dua when Sighting the New Moon

اَللّهُمَّ أَهِلَّهُ عَلَيْنَا بِالْيُمْنِ وَالْإِيمَانِ وَالسَّلَامَةِ وَالْإِسْلَامِ وَالتَّوْفِيقِ لِمَا تُحِبُّ وَتَرْضَى رَبِّي وَرَبُّكَ اللّهُ

ALLAAHUMMA AHILLAHU 'ALAINAA BIL-AMNI WAL-EEMAANI, WAS-SALAAMATI WAL-ISLAAMI, WAT-TAWFEEQI LIMAA TUHIBBU RABBANAA WA TARDHAA, RABBUNAA WA RABBUKALLAAHU.

"O Allah, let the crescent moon appear over us with security and Iman; with peace and Islam; and with ability, for us to practice such actions which you love.

(O Moon) your creator and my creator is Allah."

Ramadan Fast Tracker

1	2	3	4	5	6
7	8	9	10	11	12
13	14	15	16	17	18
19	20	21	22	23	24
25	26	27	28	29	30

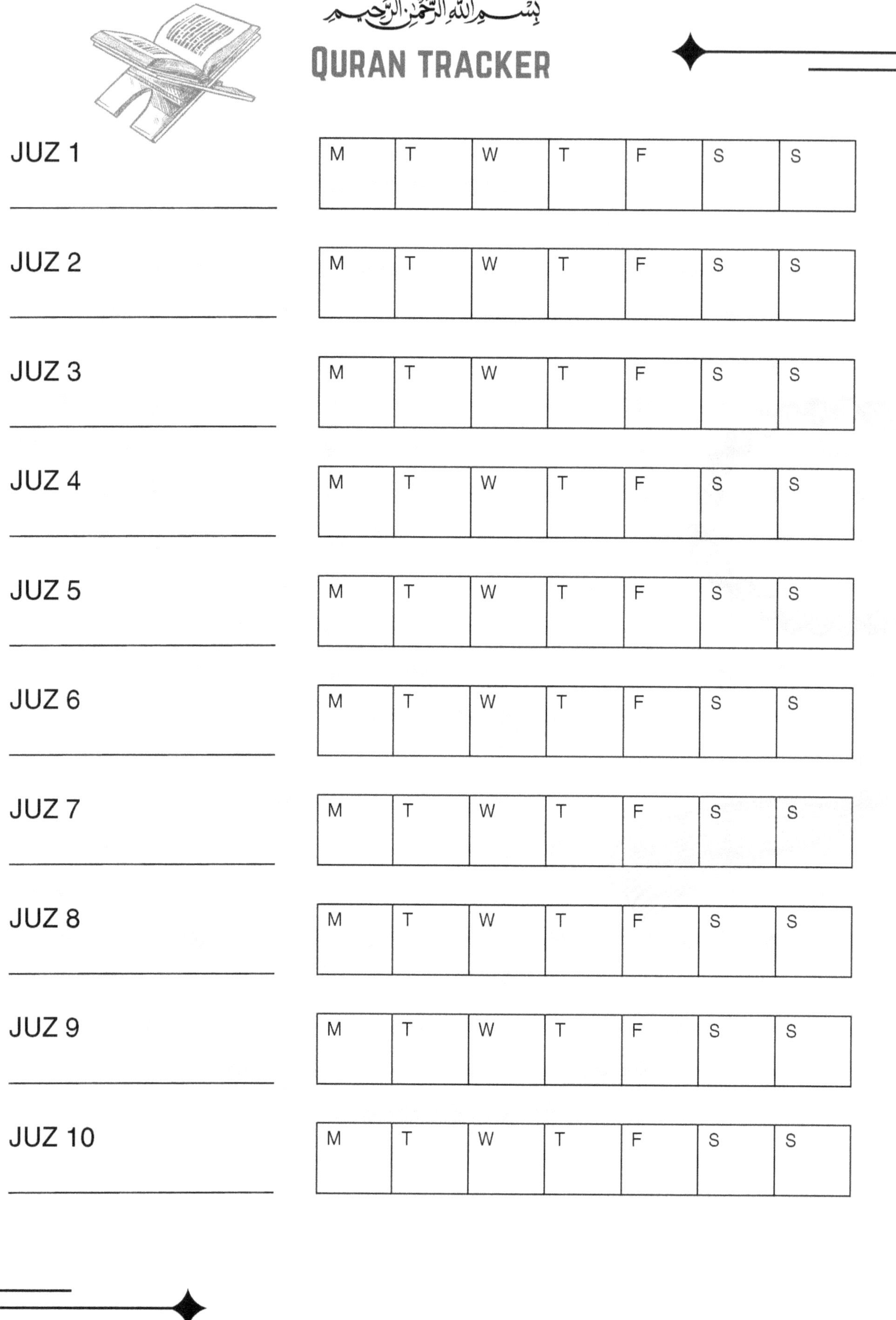

QURAN TRACKER

JUZ 1	M	T	W	T	F	S	S
_______________							

JUZ 2	M	T	W	T	F	S	S
_______________							

JUZ 3	M	T	W	T	F	S	S
_______________							

JUZ 4	M	T	W	T	F	S	S
_______________							

JUZ 5	M	T	W	T	F	S	S
_______________							

JUZ 6	M	T	W	T	F	S	S
_______________							

JUZ 7	M	T	W	T	F	S	S
_______________							

JUZ 8	M	T	W	T	F	S	S
_______________							

JUZ 9	M	T	W	T	F	S	S
_______________							

JUZ 10	M	T	W	T	F	S	S
_______________							

بِسْمِ اللهِ الرَّحْمَنِ الرَّحِيمِ

QURAN TRACKER

JUZ 11

M	T	W	T	F	S	S

JUZ12

M	T	W	T	F	S	S

JUZ 13

M	T	W	T	F	S	S

JUZ 14

M	T	W	T	F	S	S

JUZ 15

M	T	W	T	F	S	S

JUZ 16

M	T	W	T	F	S	S

JUZ 17

M	T	W	T	F	S	S

JUZ 18

M	T	W	T	F	S	S

JUZ 19

M	T	W	T	F	S	S

JUZ 20

M	T	W	T	F	S	S

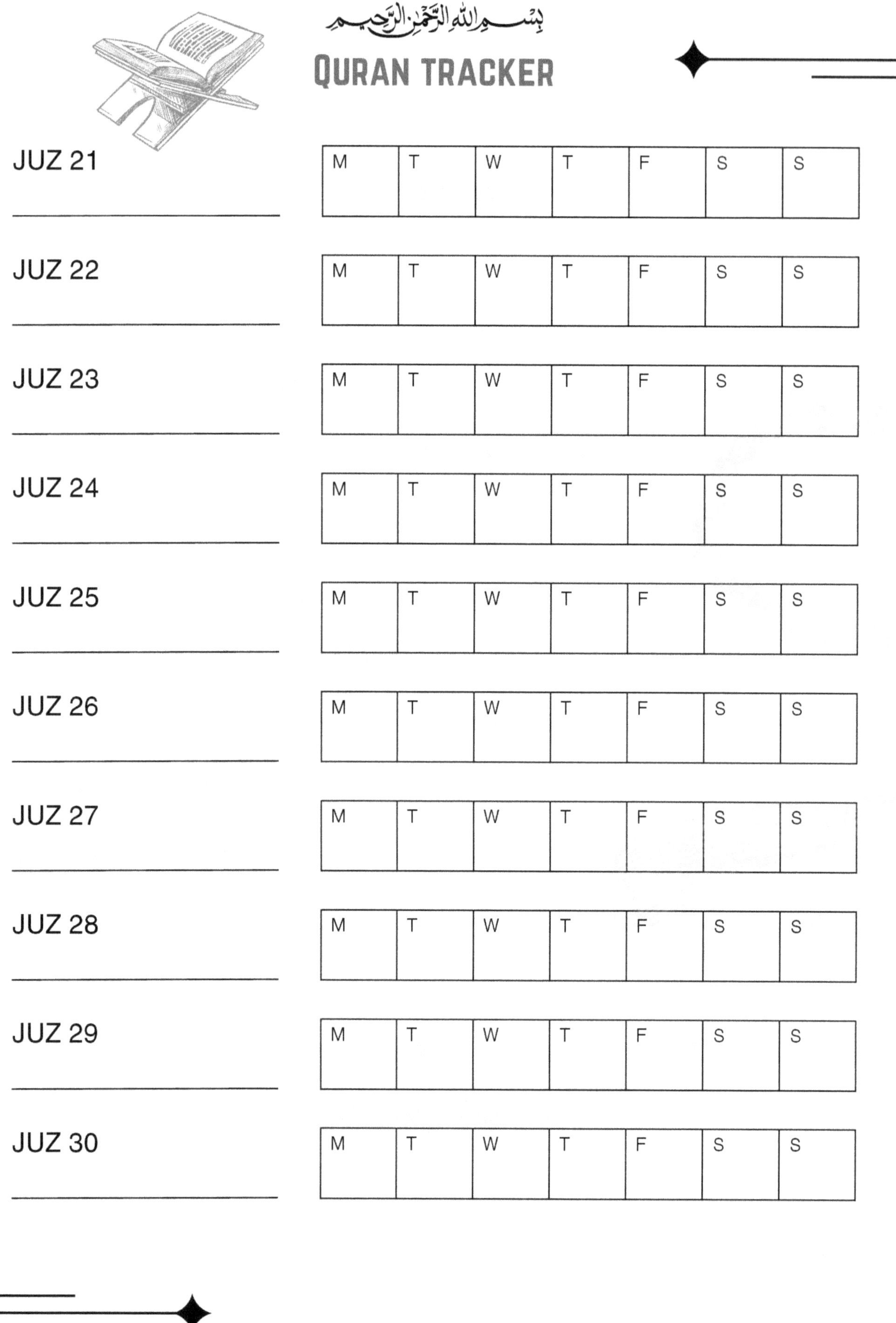

QURAN TRACKER

JUZ 21

M	T	W	T	F	S	S

JUZ 22

M	T	W	T	F	S	S

JUZ 23

M	T	W	T	F	S	S

JUZ 24

M	T	W	T	F	S	S

JUZ 25

M	T	W	T	F	S	S

JUZ 26

M	T	W	T	F	S	S

JUZ 27

M	T	W	T	F	S	S

JUZ 28

M	T	W	T	F	S	S

JUZ 29

M	T	W	T	F	S	S

JUZ 30

M	T	W	T	F	S	S

30 Days
Tarawih Challenge

Day 1	Day 2	Day 3	Day 4	Day 5	Day 6
Day 7	Day 8	Day 9	Day 10	Day 11	Day 12
Day 13	Day 14	Day 15	Day 16	Day 17	Day 18
Day 19	Day 20	Day 21	Day 22	Day 23	Day 24
Day 25	Day 26	Day 27	Day 28	Day 29	Day 30

May Allah Make it Easy

DUA FOR TARAWEEH

سُبْحَان ذِي الْمُلْكِ وَالْمَلَكُوتِ سُبْحَان ذِي الْعِزَّةِ وَ الْعَظَمةِ وَالْهَيْبَةِ وَالْقُدْرَةِ وَالْكِبْرِيَاءِ وَالْجَبَرُوتِ سُبْحَان الْمَلِكِ الْحَيِ الَّذِي لَا يَنَامُ وَ لَا يَمُوتُ سُبُّوحٌ قُدُّوسٌ رَبُّنَا وَ رَبُّ الْمَلَائِكَةِ وَ الرُّوحِ اللَّهُمَّ أَجِرْنَا مِنَ النَّارِ يَا مُجِيرُ يَا مُجِيرُ يَا مُجِيرُ

"SubHaana dhil-mulki wal-malakoot, subHaana dhil-'izzati wal-'azmati wal-haybati wal-qudrati wal-kibri-yaa 'i wal-jabaroot, subhaanal malikil Hayyil ladhi laa yanaamu wa laa yamoot, subbu- Hun quddusun rabbunaa wa rabbul-malaa 'ikati war-ruH, Allaahum- ma ajirnaa minan naar, yaa mujiru, yaa mujiru, yaa mujir"

"Glory be to the Owner of the Kingdom of the earth and the heavens. Glory be to He who commands Respect and Honour and Magnificence & Awe and Power and Greatness and Omnipotence. Glory be to the Sovereign, the Ever-living. Who does not sleep nor die. He is the Most Praised, the Most Holy, Our Lord and the Lord of all the Angels and the Spirit (Jibraeel A.S). O Allah! Save us from the Fire of Hell. O Protector! O Protector! O Protector!" Al-Bukhari 7/158.

SUHUR DUA
DUAS FOR STARTING THE FAST

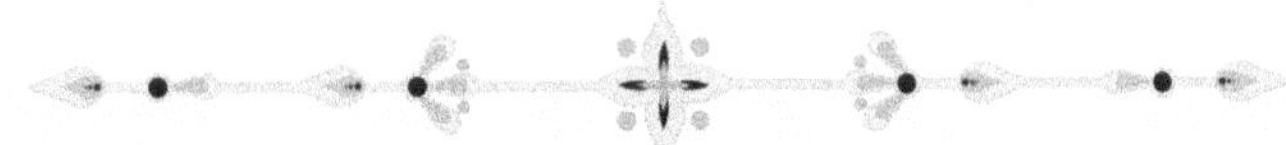

اللَّهُمَّ أَصُوْمُ لَكَ فَاغْفِرْ لِي مَا قَدَّمْتُ وَمَا أَخَرْتُ

ALLAHUMMA ASUMU LAKA FAGH FIR-LI MA QAD-DAMTU WA-MA AKH-KHARTU

O Allah! I shall fast for Your sake, so forgive my future and past sins.

بِصَوْمِ غَدٍ نَوَيْتُ مِنْ شَهْرِ رَمَضَان

BI-SAWMI GHADIN NAWAIYTU MIN SHAHRI RAMADHAN

I intend to keep the fast for tomorrow in the month of Ramadhan.

IFTAR DUA
DUAS FOR BREAKING THE FAST

اللَّهُمَّ لَكَ صُمْتُ وَبِكَ آمَنْتُ وَعَلَى رِزْقِكَ أَفْطَرْتُ

ALLAHUMMA LAKA SUMTU WA BIKA
AAMANTU WA ʼALA RIZQ-IKA AFTARTU

O Allah! I shall fast for Your sake, so

forgive my future and past sins.

Asma Ul Husna
My 30 Days with the Names of Allah

And to Allah belong the Most Beautiful Names, so call upon Him by them .

(Qur'an 7:180)

KNOWING ALLAH IS THE GREATEST JOURNEY OF THE HEART.

EACH NAME REVEALS HIS MERCY, POWER, WISDOM, AND CLOSENESS.

THIS RAMADAN, REFLECT ON ONE NAME EACH DAY—

NOT TO MEMORISE, BUT TO FEEL, CALL, AND TRUST HIM MORE DEEPLY.

GENTLE INSTRUCTION BOX:

READ THE NAME

REFLECT QUIETLY

MAKE A SIMPLE DUA

NOTICE ALLAH IN YOUR DAY

NAME	TRANSLITERATION	MEANING	REFLECTION
ٱلرَّحْمَٰنُ	AR-RAḤMĀN THE ENTIRELY MERCIFUL	AR-RAḤMĀN SHOWS MERCY TO ALL OF CREATION WITHOUT DISTINCTION.	THIS NAME REMINDS ME THAT ALLAH'S MERCY SURROUNDS EVERYTHING.
ٱلرَّحِيمُ	AR-RAḤĪM THE ESPECIALLY MERCIFUL	AR-RAḤĪM SHOWS SPECIAL MERCY TO THE BELIEVERS, ESPECIALLY IN THE HEREAFTER.	THIS NAME REMINDS ME THAT ALLAH'S MERCY IS CLOSE TO ME.
ٱلْمَلِكُ	AL-MALIK THE KING AND OWNER OF DOMINION	AL-MALIK HAS COMPLETE AUTHORITY OVER ALL THAT EXISTS.	THIS NAME REMINDS ME THAT EVERYTHING BELONGS TO ALLAH.
ٱلْقُدُّوسُ	AL-QUDDŪS THE ABSOLUTELY PURE	AL-QUDDŪS IS FREE FROM ALL IMPERFECTIONS AND FAULTS.	THIS NAME REMINDS ME TO PURIFY MY HEART AND ACTIONS.
ٱلسَّلَامُ	AS-SALĀM THE SOURCE OF PEACE	AS-SALĀM IS FREE FROM ALL DEFECTS AND GRANTS PEACE AND SAFETY.	THIS NAME REMINDS ME THAT TRUE PEACE COMES FROM ALLAH.
ٱلْمُؤْمِنُ	AL-MU'MIN THE GRANTER OF SECURITY AND FAITH	AL-MU'MIN GRANTS SAFETY, REASSURANCE, AND STRENGTHENS THE FAITH OF BELIEVERS.	THIS NAME REMINDS ME THAT MY HEART FEELS SECURE WITH ALLAH.
ٱلْمُهَيْمِنُ	AL-MUHAYMIN THE GUARDIAN, THE WITNESS, THE OVERSEER	AL-MUHAYMIN WATCHES OVER ALL CREATION WITH COMPLETE AWARENESS AND PROTECTION.	THIS NAME REMINDS ME THAT ALLAH IS ALWAYS WATCHING OVER ME.

NAME	TRANSLITERATION	MEANING	REFLECTION
ٱلْعَزِيزُ	**AL-ʿAZĪZ** THE ALL-MIGHTY, THE INVINCIBLE	AL-ʿAZĪZ POSSESSES COMPLETE POWER AND HONOUR. NOTHING CAN OVERCOME HIM, AND ALL STRENGTH BELONGS TO HIM ALONE.	THIS NAME REMINDS ME THAT TRUE STRENGTH COMES ONLY FROM ALLAH.
ٱلْجَبَّارُ	**AL-JABBĀR** THE COMPELLER, THE RESTORER	AL-JABBĀR ENFORCES HIS WILL WITH JUSTICE AND RESTORES WHAT IS BROKEN, HEALING HEARTS AND SITUATIONS.	THIS NAME REMINDS ME THAT ALLAH CAN MEND WHAT FEELS SHATTERED.
ٱلْمُتَكَبِّرُ	**AL-MUTAKABBIR** THE SUPREMELY GREAT	AL-MUTAKABBIR IS EXALTED ABOVE ALL IMPERFECTIONS AND FALSE GREATNESS.	THIS NAME REMINDS ME TO REMOVE PRIDE FROM MY HEART.
ٱلْخَٰلِقُ	**AL-KHĀLIQ** THE CREATOR	AL-KHĀLIQ CREATES EVERYTHING WITH PERFECT MEASURE AND WISDOM.	THIS NAME REMINDS ME THAT ALLAH CREATED ME WITH PURPOSE.
ٱلْبَارِئُ	**AL-BĀRI'** THE EVOLVER	AL-BĀRI' BRINGS CREATION INTO EXISTENCE IN PERFECT FORM, FREE FROM FLAW OR IMBALANCE.	THIS NAME REMINDS ME THAT ALLAH SHAPED ME BEAUTIFULLY.
ٱلْمُصَوِّرُ	**AL-MUṢAWWIR** THE FASHIONER	AL-MUṢAWWIR GIVES EVERY CREATION ITS UNIQUE SHAPE AND APPEARANCE.	THIS NAME REMINDS ME TO APPRECIATE ALLAH'S DESIGN.
ٱلْغَفَّارُ	**AL-GHAFFĀR** THE CONSTANT FORGIVER	AL-GHAFFĀR REPEATEDLY FORGIVES SINS WHEN ONE SINCERELY REPENTS.	THIS NAME REMINDS ME NEVER TO DESPAIR OF ALLAH'S MERCY.

Reflection with Asma - Ul - Husna

RAMADAN DAY____

TODAY THE NAME ___________
REMINDS ME THAT....

I FELT ALLAH'S MERCY
WHEN ...

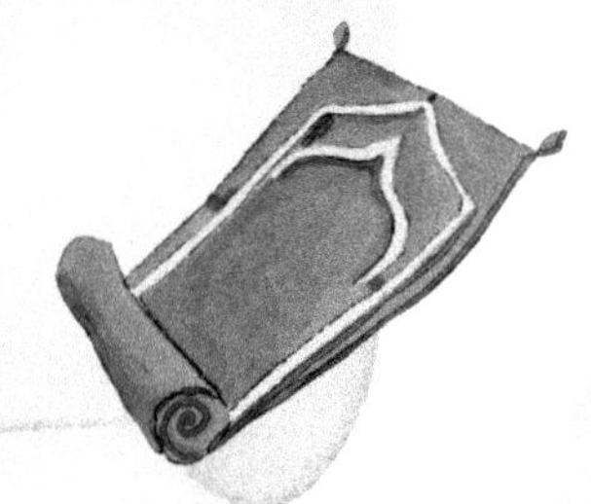

NAMES I RECITED TODAY

I NEED THIS NAME IN
MY LIFE BECAUSE...

MY FEELING TODAY

NAME	TRANSLITERATION	MEANING	REFLECTION
ٱلْقَهَّارُ	AL-QAHHĀR THE SUBDUER	AL-QAHHĀR HAS ABSOLUTE CONTROL OVER ALL CREATION; NOTHING ESCAPES HIS AUTHORITY	THIS NAME REMINDS ME THAT ALLAH IS GREATER THAN EVERY FEAR.
ٱلْوَهَّابُ	AL-WAHHĀB THE BESTOWER	AL-WAHHĀB GIVES FREELY WITHOUT EXPECTING ANYTHING IN RETURN.	THIS NAME REMINDS ME THAT EVERY BLESSING IS A GIFT FROM ALLAH.
ٱلرَّزَّاقُ	AR-RAZZĀQ THE PROVIDER	AR-RAZZĀQ PROVIDES SUSTENANCE FOR EVERY CREATURE, SEEN AND UNSEEN.	THIS NAME REMINDS ME TO TRUST ALLAH FOR MY PROVISION.
ٱلْفَتَّاحُ	AL-FATTĀḤ THE OPENER	AL-FATTĀḤ OPENS DOORS OF MERCY, GUIDANCE, AND SOLUTIONS.	THIS NAME REMINDS ME THAT ALLAH OPENS WAYS I CANNOT SEE.
ٱلْعَلِيمُ	AL-ʿALĪM THE ALL-KNOWING	AL-ʿALĪM KNOWS EVERYTHING—PAST, PRESENT, FUTURE, AND WHAT LIES IN HEARTS.	THIS NAME REMINDS ME THAT ALLAH UNDERSTANDS ME COMPLETELY.
ٱلْقَابِضُ	AL-QĀBIḌ THE WITHHOLDER	AL-QĀBIḌ WITHHOLDS WITH WISDOM, NEVER INJUSTICE.	THIS NAME REMINDS ME TO BE PATIENT DURING HARDSHIP.
ٱلْبَاسِطُ	AL-BĀSIṬ THE EXPANDER	AL-BĀSIṬ GRANTS RELIEF AND ABUNDANCE AT THE RIGHT TIME.	THIS NAME REMINDS ME THAT EASE FOLLOWS DIFFICULTY.

NAME	TRANSLITERATION	MEANING	REFLECTION
ٱلْخَافِضُ	**AL-KHĀFIḌ** THE ABASER	AL-KHĀFIḌ LOWERS THOSE WHO ACT WITH ARROGANCE AND WRONGDOING.	THIS NAME REMINDS ME TO STAY HUMBLE.
ٱلرَّافِعُ	**AR-RĀFIʿ** THE EXALTER	AR-RĀFIʿ RAISES PEOPLE IN RANK THROUGH FAITH AND RIGHTEOUSNESS.	THIS NAME REMINDS ME THAT ALLAH ELEVATES WHOM HE WILLS.
ٱلْمُعِزُّ	**AL-MUʿIZZ** THE GIVER OF HONOUR	AL-MUʿIZZ GRANTS DIGNITY, STRENGTH, AND RESPECT.	THIS NAME REMINDS ME THAT HONOUR COMES FROM ALLAH ALONE.
ٱلْمُذِلُّ	**AL-MUDHILL** THE GIVER OF HUMILIATION	AL-MUDHILL HUMBLES THOSE WHO REJECT TRUTH AND JUSTICE.	THIS NAME REMINDS ME TO SEEK HONOUR THROUGH OBEDIENCE.
ٱلسَّمِيعُ	**AS-SAMĪʿ** THE ALL-HEARING	AS-SAMĪʿ HEARS EVERY SOUND, EVERY WHISPER, AND EVERY UNSPOKEN PRAYER.	THIS NAME REMINDS ME THAT ALLAH HEARS ME EVEN WHEN I SPEAK SILENTLY.
ٱلْبَصِيرُ	**AL-BAṢĪR** THE ALL-SEEING	AL-BAṢĪR SEES EVERYTHING—OPEN AND HIDDEN, SMALL AND GREAT.	THIS NAME REMINDS ME THAT ALLAH SEES MY INTENTIONS.
ٱلْحَكَمُ	**AL-ḤAKAM** THE PERFECT JUDGE	AL-ḤAKAM JUDGES WITH COMPLETE JUSTICE AND WISDOM.	THIS NAME REMINDS ME TO TRUST ALLAH'S DECISION

Reflection with Asma - Ul - Husna

RAMADAN DAY____

TODAY THE NAME ___________

REMINDS ME THAT....

I FELT ALLAH'S MERCY

WHEN ...

NAMES I RECITED TODAY

I NEED THIS NAME IN

MY LIFE BECAUSE...

MY FEELING TODAY

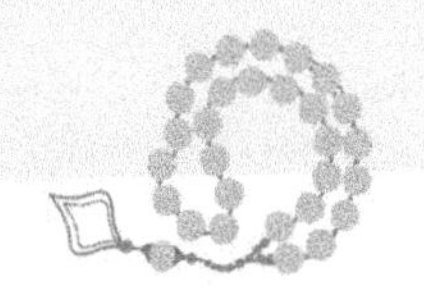

NAME	TRANSLITERATION	MEANING	REFLECTION
ٱلْعَدْلُ	AL-'ADL THE UTTERLY JUST	HE IS THE EMBODIMENT OF JUSTICE WHO NEVER WRONGS ANYONE.	THIS REMINDS ME TO BE FAIR IN MY DEALINGS AND TRUST THAT HE WILL SETTLE ALL ACCOUNTS PERFECTLY.
ٱللَّطِيفُ	AL-LATĪF THE MOST GENTLE, THE SUBTLE ONE	HE IS SO SUBTLE THAT HE IS IMPERCEPTIBLE, YET HE IS KIND AND GENTLE TOWARD HIS SERVANTS.	THIS TEACHES ME TO NOTICE THE SMALL, HIDDEN BLESSINGS IN MY LIFE.
ٱلْخَبِيرُ	AL-KHABĪR THE ALL-AWARE	HE KNOWS THE INTERNAL REALITY OF ALL THINGS, INCLUDING THE SECRETS OF THE HEART.	I SHOULD REMAIN MINDFUL THAT NOTHING I THINK OR FEEL IS HIDDEN FROM HIM.
ٱلْحَلِيمُ	AL-ḤALĪM THE MOST FORBEARING	HE IS PATIENT AND DOES NOT PUNISH HIS SERVANTS IMMEDIATELY FOR THEIR MISTAKES.	THIS ENCOURAGES ME TO BE PATIENT WITH OTHERS AND SEEK HIS FORGIVENESS CONSTANTLY.
ٱلْعَظِيمُ	AL-'AẒĪM THE MAGNIFICENT, THE SUPREME	HE IS INFINITELY GRAND AND BEYOND ALL HUMAN COMPREHENSION.	THIS HUMBLES ME AND REMINDS ME OF MY SMALLNESS IN HIS VAST CREATION.
ٱلْغَفُورُ	AL-GHAFŪR THE GREAT FORGIVER	HE FORGIVES SINS REPEATEDLY AND HIDES THE FAULTS OF HIS SERVANTS.	NO MATTER HOW MANY TIMES I SLIP, I CAN ALWAYS RETURN TO HIS FORGIVENESS.
ٱلشَّكُورُ	ASH-SHAKŪR THE MOST APPRECIATIVE	HE REWARDS EVEN THE SMALLEST GOOD DEED WITH AN ABUNDANT REWARD.	THIS MOTIVATES ME TO NEVER BELITTLE A GOOD DEED, NO MATTER HOW SMALL IT SEEMS.

NAME	TRANSLITERATION	MEANING	REFLECTION
ٱلْعَلِيُّ	**AL-'ALĪ** THE MOST HIGH, THE EXALTED	HE IS ABOVE EVERYTHING IN RANK, POWER, AND ESSENCE.	THIS REMINDS ME THAT TRUE POWER BELONGS ONLY TO HIM.
ٱلْكَبِيرُ	**AL-KABĪR** THE MOST GREAT	HE IS THE GREATEST, WHOSE GREATNESS IS INCOMPARABLE AND INFINITE.	WHEN FACING "BIG" PROBLEMS, I REMEMBER THAT ALLAH IS GREATER THAN ANYTHING I FEAR.
ٱلْحَفِيظُ	**AL-ḤAFĪẒ** THE PRESERVER, EDFUL AND ALL-PROTECTING	HE PROTECTS AND PRESERVES EVERYTHING IN EXISTENCE FROM DESTRUCTION.	I FEEL SAFE KNOWING THAT HE IS THE ULTIMATE GUARDIAN OF MY SOUL AND LIFE.
ٱلْمُقِيتُ	**AL-MUQĪT** THE SUSTAINER, THE MAINTAINER	HE PROVIDES PHYSICAL AND SPIRITUAL NOURISHMENT TO ALL LIVING BEINGS	I TRUST HIM TO PROVIDE EXACTLY WHAT I NEED TO SURVIVE AND GROW.
ٱلْحَسِيبُ	**AL-ḤASĪB** THE RECKONER	HE IS SUFFICIENT AS A SUSTAINER AND WILL TAKE ACCOUNT OF ALL DEEDS.	KNOWING HE IS ENOUGH FOR ME HELPS ME LET GO OF THE NEED FOR OTHERS' APPROVAL.
ٱلْجَلِيلُ	**AL-JALĪL** THE MAJESTIC	HE IS THE OWNER OF MAJESTY AND GLORY.	THIS NAME INSPIRES AWE AND REVERENCE IN MY HEART DURING PRAYER.
ٱلْكَرِيمُ	**AL-KARĪM** THE MOST GENEROUS	HE GIVES WITHOUT BEING ASKED AND WITHOUT EXPECTING ANYTHING IN RETURN.	THIS ENCOURAGES ME TO BE GENEROUS WITH MY TIME AND RESOURCES.

Reflection with Asma - Ul - Husna

RAMADAN DAY____

TODAY THE NAME __________

REMINDS ME THAT....

I FELT ALLAH'S MERCY

WHEN ...

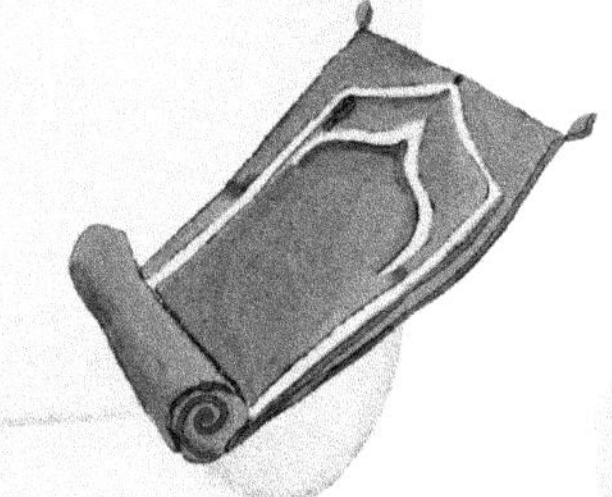

NAMES I RECITED TODAY

I NEED THIS NAME IN

MY LIFE BECAUSE...

MY FEELING TODAY

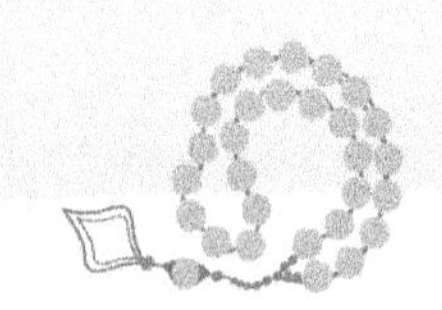

NAME	TRANSLITERATION	MEANING	REFLECTION
ٱلرَّقِيبُ	AR-RAQĪB THE WATCHFUL	HE OBSERVES EVERYTHING AND NEVER MISSES A SINGLE DETAIL.	THIS AWARENESS HELPS ME STAY AWAY FROM WRONGDOING, EVEN WHEN I AM ALONE.
ٱلْمُجِيبُ	AL-MUJĪB THE RESPONSIVE ONE	HE RESPONDS TO EVERY PRAYER AND CALL OF HIS SERVANTS.	THIS GIVES ME THE CONFIDENCE TO ALWAYS ASK HIM FOR HELP, KNOWING HE HEARS ME.
ٱلْوَاسِعُ	AL-WĀSIʿ THE ALL-ENCOMPASSING / THE BOUNDLESS	HIS MERCY, KNOWLEDGE, AND POWER HAVE NO LIMITS.	THIS TEACHES ME THAT HIS DOORS OF MERCY ARE ALWAYS OPEN, NO MATTER MY PAST.
ٱلْحَكِيمُ	AL-ḤAKĪM THE ALL-WISE	EVERYTHING HE DECREES IS DONE WITH PERFECT WISDOM AND PURPOSE.	I ACCEPT HIS PLAN FOR ME, EVEN WHEN I DON'T UNDERSTAND IT.
ٱلْوَدُودُ	AL-WADŪD THE MOST LOVING	HE IS THE SOURCE OF ALL LOVE AND LOVES HIS RIGHTEOUS SERVANTS.	THIS NAME WARMS MY HEART, REMINDING ME THAT I AM LOVED BY MY CREATOR.
ٱلْمَجِيدُ	AL-MAJĪD THE GLORIOUS / THE MOST HONORABLE	HE IS FULL OF GLORY AND DESERVES ALL PRAISE.	THIS REMINDS ME TO LIVE A LIFE THAT HONORS THE ONE WHO CREATED ME.
ٱلْبَاعِثُ	AL-BĀʿITH THE INFUSER OF NEW LIFE, THE RESURRECTOR	HE WHO GIVES LIFE TO THE DEAD ON THE DAY OF JUDGMENT AND AWAKENS THE SOULS OF PEOPLE.	THIS REMINDS ME THAT THIS LIFE IS TEMPORARY AND I WILL BE HELD ACCOUNTABLE FOR MY CHOICES

NAME	TRANSLITERATION	MEANING	REFLECTION
ٱلشَّهِيدُ	AS-SHAHĪD THE ALL-WITNESSING	HE FROM WHOM NOTHING IS HIDDEN AND WHO WITNESSES EVERYTHING IN THE HEAVENS AND ON EARTH.	KNOWING HE IS ALWAYS WATCHING ENCOURAGES ME TO BE TRUTHFUL IN MY ACTIONS, EVEN WHEN NO ONE ELSE SEES.
ٱلْحَقُّ	AL-ḤAQQ THE ABSOLUTE TRUTH	THE ONLY TRUE REALITY; HIS EXISTENCE IS CERTAIN AND HIS WORD IS THE ULTIMATE TRUTH.	IN A WORLD OF CONFUSION, I FIND STABILITY BY HOLDING ONTO THE TRUTH HE HAS PROVIDED.
ٱلْوَكِيلُ	AL-WAKĪL THE TRUSTEE, THE DISPOSER OF AFFAIRS	THE ONE WHO IS RELIED UPON AND WHO MANAGES THE AFFAIRS OF ALL HIS CREATURES WITH PERFECT CARE.	I CAN LET GO OF MY ANXIETIES BY LEAVING MY RESULTS TO THE BEST OF DISPOSERS.
ٱلْقَوِيُّ	AL-QAWIYY THE ALL-STRONG	THE ONE WITH COMPLETE AND PERFECT POWER THAT NEVER WEAKENS.	WHEN I FEEL WEAK OR OVERWHELMED, I TURN TO THE SOURCE OF ALL STRENGTH
ٱلْمَتِينُ	AL-MATĪN THE FIRM, THE STEADFAST	WHOSE STRENGTH IS UNWAVERING AND WHOSE POWER IS SOLID AND CONSTANT	THIS TEACHES ME TO BE FIRM AND STEADFAST IN MY FAITH AND PRINCIPLES.
ٱلْوَلِيُّ	AL-WALIYY THE PROTECTOR, THE GUARDIAN	THE SUPPORTIVE FRIEND AND GUARDIAN OF THE BELIEVERS.	I AM NEVER TRULY ALONE BECAUSE ALLAH IS MY CLOSEST ALLY AND PROTECTOR.
ٱلْحَمِيدُ	AL-HAMĪD THE PRAISEWORTHY, THE MOST PRAISED	THE ONLY ONE WHO IS TRULY DESERVING OF ALL PRAISE AND GRATITUDE.	EVERY BLESSING I HAVE IS A REASON TO PRAISE HIM, REGARDLESS OF MY CURRENT SITUATION

Reflection with Asma - Ul - Husna

RAMADAN DAY___

I FELT ALLAH'S MERCY
WHEN ...

TODAY THE NAME ___________
REMINDS ME THAT....

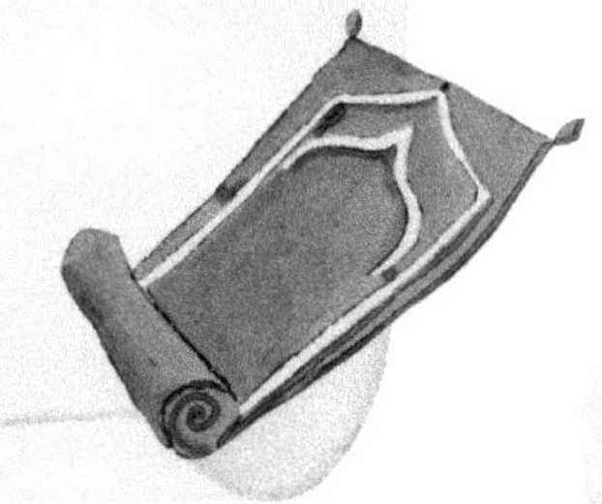

NAMES I RECITED TODAY

I NEED THIS NAME IN
MY LIFE BECAUSE...

MY FEELING TODAY

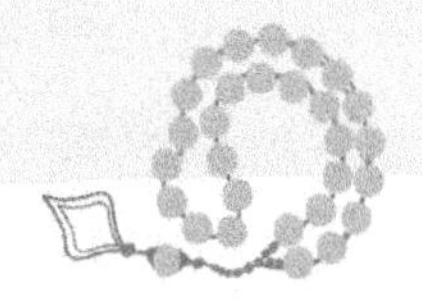

NAME	TRANSLITERATION	MEANING	REFLECTION
ٱلْحَمِيدُ	AL-ḤAMĪD THE PRAISEWORTHY, THE MOST PRAISED	THE ONLY ONE WHO IS TRULY DESERVING OF ALL PRAISE AND GRATITUDE.	EVERY BLESSING I HAVE IS A REASON TO PRAISE HIM, REGARDLESS OF MY CURRENT SITUATION.
ٱلْمُحْصِي	AL-MUHṢĪ THE ALL-ENUMERATING, THE COUNTER	HE WHO COUNTS AND RECORDS EVERY SINGLE THING IN EXISTENCE, NO MATTER HOW SMALL.	EVERY GOOD INTENTION AND TINY EFFORT I MAKE IS RECOGNIZED AND RECORDED BY HIM
ٱلْمُبْدِئُ	AL-MUBDI' THE ORIGINATOR, THE INITIATOR	HE WHO STARTED THE CREATION FROM NOTHING WITHOUT A PREVIOUS MODEL.	HE CAN CREATE NEW BEGINNINGS FOR ME EVEN WHEN I FEEL LIKE THINGS HAVE REACHED AN END.
ٱلْمُعِيدُ	AL-MUʿĪD THE ALL-STRONG	HE WHO BRINGS BACK THE CREATION AFTER IT HAS PASSED AWAY.	THIS GIVES ME HOPE THAT WHAT I HAVE LOST CAN BE RESTORED BY HIS WILL.
ٱلْمُحْيِي	AL-MUḤYĪ THE GIVER OF LIFE	HE WHO GIVES LIFE AND BRINGS THE DEAD TO LIFE.	I ASK HIM TO BRING LIFE TO MY HEART AND MY FAITH WHENEVER THEY FEEL TIRED.
ٱلْمُمِيتُ	AL-MUMĪT THE CREATOR OF DEATH	HE WHO DECREES THE END OF PHYSICAL LIFE FOR ALL LIVING BEINGS.	THIS REMINDS ME OF THE REALITY OF DEATH AND ENCOURAGES ME TO PREPARE FOR THE HEREAFTER.
ٱلْحَيُّ	AL-ḤAYY THE EVER-LIVING	HE WHOSE LIFE IS ETERNAL, WITH NO BEGINNING AND NO END.	I RELY ON THE ONE WHO NEVER DIES, WHILE ALL OTHER THINGS IN THIS WORLD EVENTUALLY FADE.

NAME	TRANSLITERATION	MEANING	REFLECTION
ٱلْقَيُّومُ	AL-QAYYŪM THE SUSTAINER, THE SELF-SUBSISTING	HE WHO EXISTS BY HIMSELF AND SUSTAINS ALL OTHER EXISTENCE.	I TRUST THAT HE IS MANAGING THE UNIVERSE PERFECTLY AT EVERY SINGLE MOMENT.
ٱلْوَاجِدُ	AL-WĀJID THE FINDER, THE PERCEIVER	WHO FINDS EVERYTHING HE SEEKS AND LACKS NOTHING.	THIS REASSURES ME THAT HE IS AWARE OF ALL MY NEEDS AND WILL PROVIDE WHAT IS MISSING
ٱلْمَاجِدُ	AL-MĀJID THE ILLUSTRIOUS, THE MAGNIFICENT	WHO IS NOBLE, GENEROUS, AND POSSESSES INFINITE GLORY	I STRIVE TO ACT WITH NOBILITY AND HONOR TO REFLECT HIS MAJESTY IN MY CHARACTER.
ٱلْوَاحِدُ	AL-WĀḤID THE ONE, THE INDIVISIBLE	HE IS UNIQUE AND INDIVISIBLE IN HIS ESSENCE AND ATTRIBUTES.	I FOCUS MY WORSHIP AND MY INTENTIONS ON HIM ALONE, AVOIDING ALL FORMS OF DISTRACTION
ٱلْأَحَدُ	AL-AḤAD THE UNIQUE, THE ONLY ONE	HE WHO STARTED THE CREATION FROM NOTHING WITHOUT A PREVIOUS MODEL.	HE CAN CREATE NEW BEGINNINGS FOR ME EVEN WHEN I FEEL LIKE THINGS HAVE REACHED AN END.
ٱلصَّمَدُ	AṢ-ṢAMAD THE ETERNAL, THE ABSOLUTE	HE WHO BRINGS BACK THE CREATION AFTER IT HAS PASSED AWAY.	THIS GIVES ME HOPE THAT WHAT I HAVE LOST CAN BE RESTORED BY HIS WILL.
ٱلْقَادِرُ	AL-QĀDIR HE OMNIPOTENT, THE ALL-ABLE	HE WHOSE STRENGTH IS UNWAVERING AND WHOSE POWER IS SOLID AND CONSTANT	THIS TEACHES ME TO BE FIRM AND STEADFAST IN MY FAITH AND PRINCIPLES.

Reflection with Asma – Ul – Husna

RAMADAN DAY____

TODAY THE NAME __________
REMINDS ME THAT....

I FELT ALLAH'S MERCY
WHEN ...

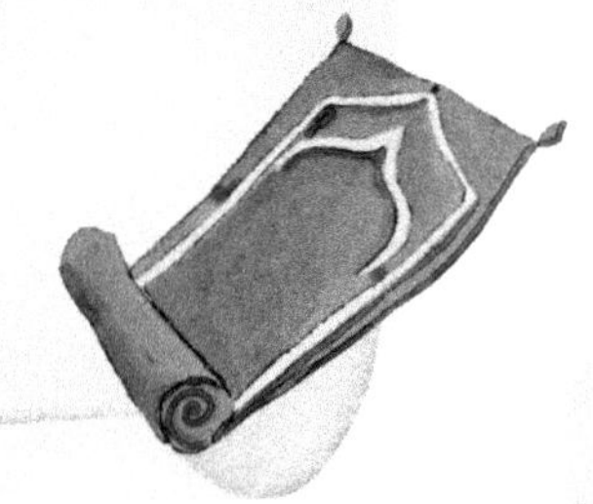

NAMES I RECITED TODAY

I NEED THIS NAME IN
MY LIFE BECAUSE...

NAME	TRANSLITERATION	MEANING	REFLECTION
ٱلْمُقْتَدِرُ	**AL-MUQTADIR** THE ALL-POWERFUL, THE DOMINANT	THE ONE WITH THE POWER TO ENFORCE HIS DECREES AND PREVAIL.	I SURRENDER TO HIS PLAN, KNOWING HIS POWER DETERMINES MY PATH FOR THE BETTER.
ٱلْمُقَدِّمُ	**AL-MUQADDIM** THE EXPEDITER, THE PROMOTER	WHO BRINGS FORWARD WHAT HE WILLS IN TIME OR RANK.	I TRUST HIS TIMING, WHETHER HE BRINGS SOMETHING TO ME EARLY OR MAKES ME WAIT.
ٱلْمُؤَخِّرُ	**AL-MU'AKHKHIR** THE DELAYER, THE POSTPONER	WHO DELAYS WHAT HE WILLS ACCORDING TO HIS PERFECT WISDOM.	WHEN THINGS ARE DELAYED, I REMAIN PATIENT, KNOWING HIS WISDOM IS AT WORK
ٱلْأَوَّلُ	**AL-AWWAL** THE FIRST, THE FOREMOST	WHO EXISTED BEFORE ANYTHING ELSE, WITH NO BEGINNING.	HE IS THE START OF MY JOURNEY AND MY ULTIMATE PRIORITY IN LIFE.
ٱلْآخِرُ	**AL-ĀKHIR** THE LAST, THE UTMOST	HE WHO REMAINS AFTER EVERYTHING ELSE HAS PERISHED, WITH NO END.	MY FINAL DESTINATION IS WITH HIM, AND I WORK TOWARD THAT MEETING.
ٱلظَّاهِرُ	**AZ-ZĀHIR** THE MANIFEST, THE ALL-SURPASSING	HE WHO IS CLEAR THROUGH HIS SIGNS AND CREATION.	I SEE HIS BEAUTY AND POWER IN EVERY PART OF THE NATURAL WORLD AROUND ME.
ٱلْبَاطِنُ	**AL-BĀṬIN** THE HIDDEN ONE, KNOWER OF THE HIDDEN	HE WHO IS HIDDEN FROM PHYSICAL SIGHT BUT CLOSE TO THE SOULS.	HE KNOWS MY INNERMOST THOUGHTS AND FEELINGS, AND HE IS CLOSER TO ME THAN MY OWN SELF.

NAME	TRANSLITERATION	MEANING	REFLECTION
ٱلْوَالِي	AL-WĀLĪ THE SOLE GOVERNOR	HE WHO MANAGES AND OWNS ALL THINGS IN EXISTENCE.	I FEEL SECURE KNOWING THE WORLD IS UNDER THE MANAGEMENT OF THE BEST OF GOVERNORS
ٱلْمُتَعَالِي	AL-MUTAʿĀLĪ THE SELF-EXALTED	HE WHO IS FAR ABOVE ANY ATTRIBUTE OF HIS CREATION.	THIS HUMBLES ME AND REMINDS ME TO ALWAYS EXALT HIM ABOVE MY OWN EGO.
ٱلْبَرُّ	AL-BARR THE SOURCE OF ALL GOODNESS	HE WHO IS KIND AND BENEFICENT TO HIS SERVANTS.	I SHOULD STRIVE TO BE A PERSON OF GOODNESS TO OTHERS, AS HE IS THE SOURCE OF ALL GOOD TO ME.
ٱلتَّوَابُ	AT-TAWWĀB THE EVER-PARDONING	HE WHO REPEATEDLY ACCEPTS THE REPENTANCE OF HIS SERVANTS.	I NEVER LOSE HOPE IN HIS MERCY, NO MATTER HOW MANY TIMES I NEED TO ASK FOR FORGIVENESS.
ٱلْمُنْتَقِمُ	AL-MUNTAQIM THE AVENGER	HE WHO BRINGS JUSTICE BY PUNISHING THOSE WHO PERSIST IN WRONGDOING.	THIS NAME REASSURES ME THAT ULTIMATE JUSTICE WILL BE SERVED FOR ALL OPPRESSION
ٱلْعَفُوُّ	AL-ʿAFŪW THE PARDONER	HE WHO WIPES OUT SINS AND REMOVES THEIR TRACES COMPLETELY.	I ASK HIM TO NOT JUST FORGIVE MY SINS, BUT TO ERASE THEM FROM MY RECORD ENTIRELY.
ٱلرَّءُوفُ	AR-RAʾŪF THE MOST KIND	HE WHO IS EXTREMELY MERCIFUL AND FULL OF PITY FOR HIS CREATION.	THIS ENCOURAGES ME TO BE GENTLE AND KIND TOWARD ALL LIVING BEINGS.

Reflection with Asma - Ul - Husna

RAMADAN DAY____

TODAY THE NAME __________

REMINDS ME THAT....

I FELT ALLAH'S MERCY WHEN ...

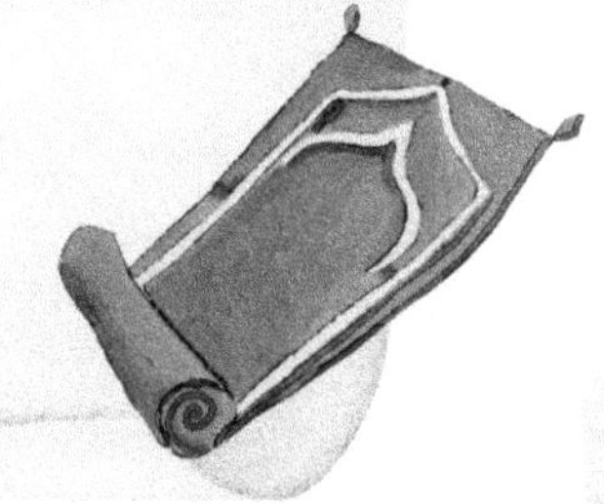

NAMES I RECITED TODAY

I NEED THIS NAME IN MY LIFE BECAUSE...

MY FEELING TODAY

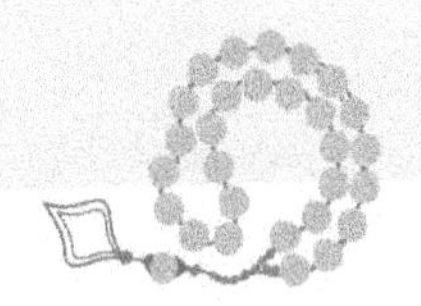

NAME	TRANSLITERATION	MEANING	REFLECTION
مَالِكُ الْمُلْكِ	MĀLIK AL-MULK MASTER OF THE DOMINION, OWNER OF THE KINGDOM	HE WHO HAS ABSOLUTE OWNERSHIP AND AUTHORITY OVER ALL CREATION.	I RECOGNIZE THAT EVERYTHING I "OWN" IN THIS LIFE IS ACTUALLY A TRUST FROM HIM.
ذُوالْجَلَالِ وَالْإِكْرَام	DHŪ AL-JALĀLI WA'L-IKRĀM POSSESSOR OF GLORY AND HONOUR	HE WHO IS THE SOURCE OF ALL GRANDEUR AND BOUNTY.	THIS NAME FILLS ME WITH AWE AND GRATITUDE, INSPIRING ME TO WORSHIP HIM WITH REVERENCE
الْمُقْسِطُ	AL-MUQSIṬ THE JUST ONE	HE WHO ACTS WITH ABSOLUTE FAIRNESS AND RESTORES RIGHTS.	I MUST BE FAIR IN MY OWN JUDGMENTS AND DEALINGS, REFLECTING HIS JUSTICE
الْجَامِعُ	AL-JĀMI' THE GATHERER, THE UNITER	HE WHO BRINGS TOGETHER ALL OF CREATION, ESPECIALLY ON THE DAY OF JUDGMENT.	THIS REMINDS ME THAT WE WILL ALL BE GATHERED BACK TO HIM, SO I SHOULD WORK TO UNITE PEOPLE IN GOODNESS
الْغَنِيُّ	AL-GHANIYY THE SELF-SUFFICIENT, THE WEALTHY	HE WHO IS PERFECTLY INDEPENDENT AND NEEDS NOTHING FROM HIS CREATION.	I REALIZE THAT MY WORSHIP DOESN'T BENEFIT HIM; IT IS FOR MY OWN SOUL'S GROWTH.
الْمُغْنِي	AL-MUGHNĪ THE ENRICHER	HE WHO PROVIDES WEALTH AND SUFFICIENCY TO WHOMEVER HE WILLS.	I TURN TO HIM FOR BOTH MATERIAL AND SPIRITUAL ENRICHMENT.
الْمَانِعُ	AL-MĀNI' THE WITHHOLDER	HE WHO PREVENTS HARM AND WITHHOLDS WHAT IS NOT GOOD FOR HIS SERVANTS.	I TRUST THAT WHEN HE SAYS "NO" TO MY REQUESTS, IT IS OUT OF HIS PROTECTION AND CARE.

NAME	TRANSLITERATION	MEANING	REFLECTION
ٱلضَّارُّ	AD-ḌĀRR THE DISTRESSER / THE AFFLICTER	WHO DECREES TRIALS AND HARDSHIPS ACCORDING TO HIS WISDOM.	HARDSHIPS ARE TESTS FROM HIM TO BRING ME CLOSER TO HIM AND REFINE MY SOUL.
ٱلنَّافِعُ	AN-NĀFI' THE PROPITIOUS / THE BENEFACTOR	WHO IS THE ONLY SOURCE OF TRUE BENEFIT AND GOODNESS.	I SEEK BENEFIT ONLY FROM HIM, KNOWING THAT NO ONE ELSE CAN TRULY HELP ME WITHOUT HIS WILL.
ٱلنُّورُ	AN-NŪR THE LIGHT / THE ILLUMINATOR	WHO GUIDES THE HEAVENS AND THE EARTH AND BRINGS LIGHT TO THE HEARTS.	I ASK HIM TO LIGHT MY PATH WHEN I AM LOST AND FILL MY HEART WITH THE LIGHT OF FAITH.
ٱلْهَادِي	AL-HĀDĪ THE GUIDE	WHO PROVIDES GUIDANCE AND LEADS HIS SERVANTS TO THE RIGHT PATH.	MY DAILY PRAYER IS FOR HIS CONTINUOUS GUIDANCE IN EVERY DECISION I MAKE.
ٱلْبَدِيعُ	AL-BADĪ' THE INCOMPARABLE ORIGINATOR	WHO CREATED EVERYTHING IN A UNIQUE AND WONDERFUL WAY.	THIS INSPIRES ME TO BE CREATIVE AND APPRECIATE THE UNIQUE BEAUTY IN HIS CREATION
ٱلْبَاقِي	AL-BĀQĪ THE EVERLASTING	WHO REMAINS FOREVER WHILE ALL OF CREATION PASSES AWAY.	I SHOULD INVEST MY TIME IN THINGS THAT WILL LAST FOR ETERNITY RATHER THAN TEMPORARY WORLDLY GAINS.
ٱلْوَارِثُ	AL-WĀRITH THE INHERITOR	TO WHOM EVERYTHING RETURNS AFTER ITS OWNERS HAVE PASSED.	I AM JUST A TEMPORARY KEEPER OF MY POSSESSIONS; THEY WILL ALL RETURN TO HIM.

NAME	TRANSLITERATION	MEANING	REFLECTION

AR-RASHĪD

ٱلرَّشِيدُ

THE GUIDE TO THE RIGHT PATH

HE WHO DIRECTS HIS SERVANTS WITH PERFECT WISDOM TOWARD THE TRUTH.

I SEEK HIS WISDOM TO MAKE THE RIGHT CHOICES AND STAY ON THE STRAIGHT PATH.

AṢ-ṢABŪR

ٱلصَّبُورُ

THE PATIENT

HE WHO IS MOST PATIENT AND DOES NOT HASTEN TO PUNISH.

I LEARN FROM HIM TO BE PATIENT WITH MYSELF AND OTHERS, TRUSTING IN HIS PERFECT TIMING

وَلِلَّهِ ٱلْأَسْمَآءُ ٱلْحُسْنَىٰ فَٱدْعُوهُ بِهَا

WA LILLĀHI AL-ASMĀ'U AL-ḤUSNĀ FA-UDʿŪHU BIHĀ

"TO ALLAH BELONG THE MOST BEAUTIFUL NAMES, SO CALL UPON HIM BY THEM."

— SURAH AL-AʿRĀF (7:180)

THROUGH THE NAMES OF ALLAH, I LEARNED TO KNOW MY RABB.

AR-RASHĪD GUIDED MY HEART WHEN CLARITY WAS DISTANT.

AṢ-ṢABŪR ALLOWED ME TO GROW WITHOUT HASTE.

EVERY NAME CARRIED MERCY, WISDOM, AND PURPOSE.

I PLACE MY TRUST IN ALLAH —

THE ONE WHOSE NAMES ARE PERFECT,

WHOSE TIMING IS FLAWLESS,

AND WHOSE GUIDANCE NEVER FAILS.

Reflection with Asma - Ul - Husna

RAMADAN DAY____

I FELT ALLAH'S MERCY
WHEN ...

TODAY THE NAME ____________
REMINDS ME THAT....

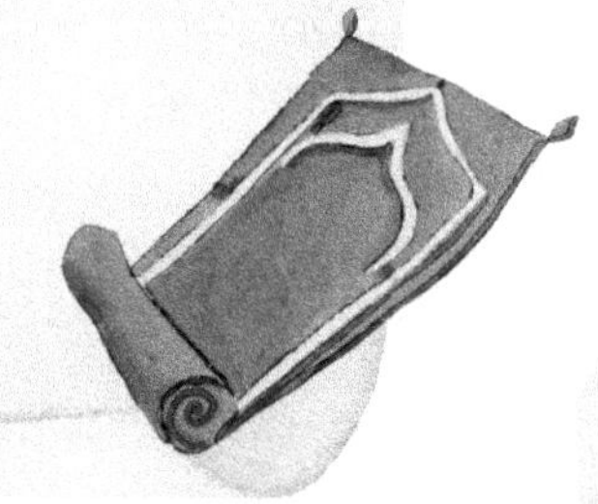

NAMES I RECITED TODAY

I NEED THIS NAME IN
MY LIFE BECAUSE...

MY FEELING TODAY

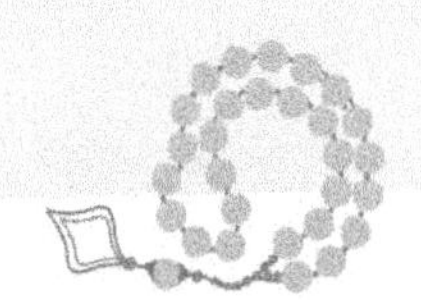

30 DAYS

RAMADAN
CHALLENGE

2026

DAY 1	DAY 2	DAY 3	DAY 4	DAY 5
READ JUZ 1-2	MEMORIZE SURAH	READ JUZ 3-4	MEMORIZE SURAH	READ JUZ 5-6
DAY 6	DAY 7	DAY 8	DAY 9	DAY 10
MEMORIZE SURAH	READ JUZ 7-8	MEMORIZE SURAH	READ JUZ 9-10	MEMORIZE SURAH
DAY 11	DAY 12	DAY 13	DAY 14	DAY 15
READ JUZ 11-12	MEMORIZE SURAH	READ JUZ 13-14	MEMORIZE SURAH	READ JUZ 15-16
DAY 16	DAY 17	DAY 18	DAY 19	DAY 20
MEMORIZE SURAH	READ JUZ 17-18	MEMORIZE SURAH	READ JUZ 19-20	MEMORIZE SURAH
DAY 21	DAY 22	DAY 23	DAY 24	DAY 25
READ JUZ 21-22	MEMORIZE SURAH	READ JUZ 23-24	MEMORIZE SURAH	READ JUZ 25-26
DAY 26	DAY 27	DAY 28	DAY 29	DAY 30
MEMORIZE SURAH	READ JUZ 27-28	MEMORIZE SURAH	READ JUZ 29-30	MEMORIZE SURAH

بِسْمِ اللّٰهِ الرَّحْمٰنِ الرَّحِيْمِ

Ramadan
Daily Planner

RAMADAN DAY:

DATE:

FASTING: ● YES ● NO

IBADAH CHECKLIST

- ○ Fasting
- ○ Fajr
- ○ Dhuhr
- ○ Asr
- ○ Maghrib
- ○ Isha

- ○ Tarawih
- ○ Witr
- ○ Dhuha
- ○ Tahajud
- ○ Rawatib
- ○ Dhikr

GOOD DEEDS

- ○ Dhikr
- ○ Dua
- ○ _______________

- ○ Sadaqah
- ○ Study

HADITH OF THE DAY

PRIORITIES

____
____
____
____

QURAN READING

Surah: _______________   Ayah: _______________

Notes:

____
____
____
____

WATER

○ ○ ○ ○ ○ ○ ○ ○

WHAT I AM GRATEFUL FOR TODAY

DAILY CHECKLIST

- ○ Morning Adhkar
- ○ Evening Adhkar
- ○ Deed Of The Day
- ○ Adhkar Before Sleep

- ○ Istighfar
- ○ Shukr
- ○ Dhikr
- ○ Charity

Ramadan
Daily Planner

RAMADAN DAY: DATE: FASTING: ● YES ◐ NO

IBADAH CHECKLIST

- ⬤ Fasting
- ⬤ Fajr
- ⬤ Dhuhr
- ⬤ Asr
- ⬤ Maghrib
- ⬤ Isha

- ⬤ Tarawih
- ⬤ Witr
- ⬤ Dhuha
- ⬤ Tahajud
- ⬤ Rawatib
- ⬤ Dhikr

GOOD DEEDS

- ⬤ Dhikr
- ⬤ Dua
- ⬤ _______________

- ⬤ Sadaqah
- ⬤ Study

HADITH OF THE DAY

PRIORITIES

____
____
____
____

QURAN READING

Surah: _____________ Ayah: _________

Notes:

____
____
____
____

WATER

⬤ ⬤ ⬤ ⬤ ⬤ ⬤ ⬤ ⬤

WHAT I AM GRATEFUL FOR TODAY

DAILY CHECKLIST

- ◯ Morning Adhkar
- ◯ Evening Adhkar
- ◯ Deed Of The Day
- ◯ Adhkar Before Sleep

- ◯ Istighfar
- ◯ Shukr
- ◯ Dhikr
- ◯ Charity

Ramadan
Daily Planner

RAMADAN DAY: | DATE: | FASTING: YES NO

IBADAH CHECKLIST

- Fasting
- Fajr
- Dhuhr
- Asr
- Maghrib
- Isha

- Tarawih
- Witr
- Dhuha
- Tahajud
- Rawatib
- Dhikr

GOOD DEEDS

- Dhikr
- Dua

- Sadaqah
- Study

- _______________

HADITH OF THE DAY

PRIORITIES

____
____
____

QURAN READING

Surah: _______________   Ayah: _______________

Notes:
____
____
____

WHAT I AM GRATEFUL FOR TODAY

WATER

DAILY CHECKLIST

- Morning Adhkar
- Evening Adhkar
- Deed Of The Day
- Adhkar Before Sleep

- Istighfar
- Shukr
- Dhikr
- Charity

Ibadah Creations

بِسْمِ اللَّهِ الرَّحْمَنِ الرَّحِيمِ

Ramadan
Daily Planner

RAMADAN DAY:

DATE:

FASTING: ◐ YES ◑ NO

IBADAH CHECKLIST

- ◯ Fasting
- ◯ Fajr
- ◯ Dhuhr
- ◯ Asr
- ◯ Maghrib
- ◯ Isha

- ◯ Tarawih
- ◯ Witr
- ◯ Dhuha
- ◯ Tahajud
- ◯ Rawatib
- ◯ Dhikr

GOOD DEEDS

- ◯ Dhikr
- ◯ Dua
- ◯ _______________

- ◯ Sadaqah
- ◯ Study

HADITH OF THE DAY

PRIORITIES

____
____
____
____

QURAN READING

Surah: _______________ Ayah: _______

Notes:

____
____
____

WATER

◯ ◯ ◯ ◯ ◯ ◯ ◯ ◯

WHAT I AM GRATEFUL FOR TODAY

DAILY CHECKLIST

- ◯ Morning Adhkar
- ◯ Evening Adhkar
- ◯ Deed Of The Day
- ◯ Adhkar Before Sleep

- ◯ Istighfar
- ◯ Shukr
- ◯ Dhikr
- ◯ Charity

Ramadan
Daily Planner

RAMADAN DAY: | DATE: | FASTING: YES NO

IBADAH CHECKLIST

- ◯ Fasting
- ◯ Fajr
- ◯ Dhuhr
- ◯ Asr
- ◯ Maghrib
- ◯ Isha

- ◯ Tarawih
- ◯ Witr
- ◯ Dhuha
- ◯ Tahajud
- ◯ Rawatib
- ◯ Dhikr

GOOD DEEDS

- ◯ Dhikr
- ◯ Dua
- ◯ _______________

- ◯ Sadaqah
- ◯ Study

HADITH OF THE DAY

PRIORITIES

____
____
____
____

QURAN READING

Surah: _____________   Ayah: _____________

Notes:
____
____
____
____

WATER

WHAT I AM GRATEFUL FOR TODAY

DAILY CHECKLIST

- ◯ Morning Adhkar
- ◯ Evening Adhkar
- ◯ Deed Of The Day
- ◯ Adhkar Before Sleep

- ◯ Istighfar
- ◯ Shukr
- ◯ Dhikr
- ◯ Charity

Ramadan
Daily Planner

RAMADAN DAY: | DATE: | FASTING: ◐ YES ◐ NO

IBADAH CHECKLIST

- ⬤ Fasting
- ⬤ Fajr
- ⬤ Dhuhr
- ⬤ Asr
- ⬤ Maghrib
- ⬤ Isha

- ⬤ Tarawih
- ⬤ Witr
- ⬤ Dhuha
- ⬤ Tahajud
- ⬤ Rawatib
- ⬤ Dhikr

GOOD DEEDS

- ⬤ Dhikr
- ⬤ Dua
- ⬤ ____________________

- ⬤ Sadaqah
- ⬤ Study

HADITH OF THE DAY

PRIORITIES

____
____
____
____

QURAN READING

Surah: ______________ Ayah: ________

Notes:
____
____
____
____

WATER

💧 💧 💧 💧 💧 💧 💧 💧

WHAT I AM GRATEFUL FOR TODAY

DAILY CHECKLIST

- ⬤ Morning Adhkar
- ⬤ Evening Adhkar
- ⬤ Deed Of The Day
- ⬤ Adhkar Before Sleep

- ⬤ Istighfar
- ⬤ Shukr
- ⬤ Dhikr
- ⬤ Charity

بِسْمِ اللهِ الرَّحْمَنِ الرَّحِيمِ

Ramadan
Daily Planner

RAMADAN DAY:

DATE:

FASTING: YES NO

IBADAH CHECKLIST

- Fasting
- Fajr
- Dhuhr
- Asr
- Maghrib
- Isha

- Tarawih
- Witr
- Dhuha
- Tahajud
- Rawatib
- Dhikr

GOOD DEEDS

- Dhikr
- Dua

- Sadaqah
- Study

- ______________________

HADITH OF THE DAY

PRIORITIES

____

____

____

____

QURAN READING

Surah: ______________   Ayah: __________

Notes:

____

____

____

____

WATER

WHAT I AM GRATEFUL FOR TODAY

DAILY CHECKLIST

- Morning Adhkar
- Evening Adhkar
- Deed Of The Day
- Adhkar Before Sleep

- Istighfar
- Shukr
- Dhikr
- Charity

Ramadan
Daily Planner

RAMADAN DAY: DATE: FASTING: ● YES ◐ NO

IBADAH CHECKLIST

- ◯ Fasting
- ◯ Fajr
- ◯ Dhuhr
- ◯ Asr
- ◯ Maghrib
- ◯ Isha

- ◯ Tarawih
- ◯ Witr
- ◯ Dhuha
- ◯ Tahajud
- ◯ Rawatib
- ◯ Dhikr

GOOD DEEDS

- ◯ Dhikr
- ◯ Dua
- ◯ __________

- ◯ Sadaqah
- ◯ Study

HADITH OF THE DAY

PRIORITIES

____
____
____
____

QURAN READING

Surah: ____________   Ayah: __________

Notes:

____
____
____
____

WATER

WHAT I AM GRATEFUL FOR TODAY

DAILY CHECKLIST

- ◯ Morning Adhkar
- ◯ Evening Adhkar
- ◯ Deed Of The Day
- ◯ Adhkar Before Sleep

- ◯ Istighfar
- ◯ Shukr
- ◯ Dhikr
- ◯ Charity

Ibadah Creations

بِسْمِ اللهِ الرَّحْمَنِ الرَّحِيمِ

Ramadan
Daily Planner

RAMADAN DAY: | DATE: | FASTING: ◐ YES ◑ NO

IBADAH CHECKLIST

- ◯ Fasting
- ◯ Fajr
- ◯ Dhuhr
- ◯ Asr
- ◯ Maghrib
- ◯ Isha

- ◯ Tarawih
- ◯ Witr
- ◯ Dhuha
- ◯ Tahajud
- ◯ Rawatib
- ◯ Dhikr

GOOD DEEDS

- ◯ Dhikr
- ◯ Dua
- ◯ _______________

- ◯ Sadaqah
- ◯ Study

HADITH OF THE DAY

PRIORITIES

____
____
____
____

QURAN READING

Surah: _____________   Ayah: _______

Notes:
____
____
____
____

WATER

WHAT I AM GRATEFUL FOR TODAY

DAILY CHECKLIST

- ◯ Morning Adhkar
- ◯ Evening Adhkar
- ◯ Deed Of The Day
- ◯ Adhkar Before Sleep

- ◯ Istighfar
- ◯ Shukr
- ◯ Dhikr
- ◯ Charity

بِسْمِ اللهِ الرَّحْمَنِ الرَّحِيمِ

Ramadan
Daily Planner

RAMADAN DAY:

DATE:

FASTING: YES NO

IBADAH CHECKLIST

- Fasting
- Fajr
- Dhuhr
- Asr
- Maghrib
- Isha

- Tarawih
- Witr
- Dhuha
- Tahajud
- Rawatib
- Dhikr

GOOD DEEDS

- Dhikr
- Dua
- ________________

- Sadaqah
- Study

QURAN READING

Surah: ________________ Ayah: ________________

Notes:

____
____
____
____

HADITH OF THE DAY

PRIORITIES

____
____
____
____

WATER

WHAT I AM GRATEFUL FOR TODAY

DAILY CHECKLIST

- Morning Adhkar
- Evening Adhkar
- Deed Of The Day
- Adhkar Before Sleep

- Istighfar
- Shukr
- Dhikr
- Charity

Ibadah Creations

Ramadan
Daily Planner

RAMADAN DAY: | DATE: | FASTING: YES NO

IBADAH CHECKLIST

- ◯ Fasting
- ◯ Fajr
- ◯ Dhuhr
- ◯ Asr
- ◯ Maghrib
- ◯ Isha
- ◯ Tarawih
- ◯ Witr
- ◯ Dhuha
- ◯ Tahajud
- ◯ Rawatib
- ◯ Dhikr

GOOD DEEDS

- ◯ Dhikr
- ◯ Dua
- ◯ Sadaqah
- ◯ Study
- ◯ ____________________

HADITH OF THE DAY

PRIORITIES

____
____
____
____

QURAN READING

Surah: ______________ Ayah: ________

Notes:
____
____
____
____

WATER

◇ ◇ ◇ ◇ ◇ ◇ ◇ ◇

WHAT I AM GRATEFUL FOR TODAY

DAILY CHECKLIST

- ◯ Morning Adhkar
- ◯ Evening Adhkar
- ◯ Deed Of The Day
- ◯ Adhkar Before Sleep
- ◯ Istighfar
- ◯ Shukr
- ◯ Dhikr
- ◯ Charity

Ramadan
Daily Planner

RAMADAN DAY:

DATE:

FASTING: YES NO

IBADAH CHECKLIST

- Fasting
- Fajr
- Dhuhr
- Asr
- Maghrib
- Isha
- Tarawih
- Witr
- Dhuha
- Tahajud
- Rawatib
- Dhikr

GOOD DEEDS

- Dhikr
- Dua
- Sadaqah
- Study
- ______________________

HADITH OF THE DAY

PRIORITIES

QURAN READING

Surah: ______________ Ayah: ______

Notes:

____
____
____
____

WATER

WHAT I AM GRATEFUL FOR TODAY

DAILY CHECKLIST

- Morning Adhkar
- Evening Adhkar
- Deed Of The Day
- Adhkar Before Sleep
- Istighfar
- Shukr
- Dhikr
- Charity

Ramadan
Daily Planner

RAMADAN DAY: **DATE:**   **FASTING:** ● YES ● NO

IBADAH CHECKLIST

- ○ Fasting
- ○ Fajr
- ○ Dhuhr
- ○ Asr
- ○ Maghrib
- ○ Isha

- ○ Tarawih
- ○ Witr
- ○ Dhuha
- ○ Tahajud
- ○ Rawatib
- ○ Dhikr

GOOD DEEDS

- ○ Dhikr
- ○ Dua
- ○ ______________________

- ○ Sadaqah
- ○ Study

HADITH OF THE DAY

PRIORITIES

____
____
____
____

QURAN READING

Surah: ______________   Ayah: ________

Notes:
____
____
____
____

WATER

WHAT I AM GRATEFUL FOR TODAY

DAILY CHECKLIST

- ○ Morning Adhkar
- ○ Evening Adhkar
- ○ Deed Of The Day
- ○ Adhkar Before Sleep

- ○ Istighfar
- ○ Shukr
- ○ Dhikr
- ○ Charity

بِسْمِ اللهِ الرَّحْمَنِ الرَّحِيمِ

Ramadan
Daily Planner

RAMADAN DAY:

DATE:

FASTING: ◑ YES ◑ NO

IBADAH CHECKLIST

- ◯ Fasting
- ◯ Fajr
- ◯ Dhuhr
- ◯ Asr
- ◯ Maghrib
- ◯ Isha
- ◯ Tarawih
- ◯ Witr
- ◯ Dhuha
- ◯ Tahajud
- ◯ Rawatib
- ◯ Dhikr

GOOD DEEDS

- ◯ Dhikr
- ◯ Dua
- ◯ Sadaqah
- ◯ Study
- ◯ ____________

HADITH OF THE DAY

PRIORITIES

____
____
____
____

QURAN READING

Surah: ____________ Ayah: ________

Notes:
____
____
____
____

WATER

◌ ◌ ◌ ◌ ◌ ◌ ◌ ◌

WHAT I AM GRATEFUL FOR TODAY

DAILY CHECKLIST

- ◯ Morning Adhkar
- ◯ Evening Adhkar
- ◯ Deed Of The Day
- ◯ Adhkar Before Sleep
- ◯ Istighfar
- ◯ Shukr
- ◯ Dhikr
- ◯ Charity

بِسْمِ اللهِ الرَّحْمَنِ الرَّحِيمِ

Ramadan
Daily Planner

RAMADAN DAY:

DATE:

FASTING: ◐ YES ◑ NO

IBADAH CHECKLIST

- ◯ Fasting
- ◯ Fajr
- ◯ Dhuhr
- ◯ Asr
- ◯ Maghrib
- ◯ Isha

- ◯ Tarawih
- ◯ Witr
- ◯ Dhuha
- ◯ Tahajud
- ◯ Rawatib
- ◯ Dhikr

GOOD DEEDS

- ◯ Dhikr
- ◯ Dua
- ◯ __________

- ◯ Sadaqah
- ◯ Study

HADITH OF THE DAY

PRIORITIES

____
____
____
____

QURAN READING

Surah: ______________ Ayah: ________

Notes:
____
____
____
____

WATER

◌ ◌ ◌ ◌ ◌ ◌ ◌ ◌

WHAT I AM GRATEFUL FOR TODAY

DAILY CHECKLIST

- ◯ Morning Adhkar
- ◯ Evening Adhkar
- ◯ Deed Of The Day
- ◯ Adhkar Before Sleep

- ◯ Istighfar
- ◯ Shukr
- ◯ Dhikr
- ◯ Charity

Ibadah Creations

Ramadan
Daily Planner

RAMADAN DAY: **DATE:**   **FASTING:** YES NO

IBADAH CHECKLIST

- Fasting
- Fajr
- Dhuhr
- Asr
- Maghrib
- Isha

- Tarawih
- Witr
- Dhuha
- Tahajud
- Rawatib
- Dhikr

GOOD DEEDS

- Dhikr
- Dua

- Sadaqah
- Study

- ___________________________

HADITH OF THE DAY

PRIORITIES

____

____

____

____

QURAN READING

Surah: ______________   Ayah: ______________

Notes:

____

____

____

____

WATER

WHAT I AM GRATEFUL FOR TODAY

DAILY CHECKLIST

- Morning Adhkar
- Evening Adhkar
- Deed Of The Day
- Adhkar Before Sleep

- Istighfar
- Shukr
- Dhikr
- Charity

Ramadan
Daily Planner

RAMADAN DAY: **DATE:**   **FASTING:** YES   NO

IBADAH CHECKLIST

- Fasting
- Fajr
- Dhuhr
- Asr
- Maghrib
- Isha
- Tarawih
- Witr
- Dhuha
- Tahajud
- Rawatib
- Dhikr

GOOD DEEDS

- Dhikr
- Dua
- Sadaqah
- Study
- _______________

HADITH OF THE DAY

PRIORITIES

QURAN READING

Surah: _______________   Ayah: _______

Notes:

____
____
____
____

WATER

WHAT I AM GRATEFUL FOR TODAY

DAILY CHECKLIST

- Morning Adhkar
- Evening Adhkar
- Deed Of The Day
- Adhkar Before Sleep
- Istighfar
- Shukr
- Dhikr
- Charity

Ramadan
Daily Planner

RAMADAN DAY: **DATE:** **FASTING:** YES NO

IBADAH CHECKLIST

- Fasting
- Fajr
- Dhuhr
- Asr
- Maghrib
- Isha
- Tarawih
- Witr
- Dhuha
- Tahajud
- Rawatib
- Dhikr

GOOD DEEDS

- Dhikr
- Dua
- Sadaqah
- Study
- __________________

HADITH OF THE DAY

PRIORITIES

____
____
____

QURAN READING

Surah: __________ Ayah: ______

Notes:
____
____
____
____

WATER

WHAT I AM GRATEFUL FOR TODAY

DAILY CHECKLIST

- Morning Adhkar
- Evening Adhkar
- Deed Of The Day
- Adhkar Before Sleep
- Istighfar
- Shukr
- Dhikr
- Charity

Ibadah Creations

بِسْمِ اللهِ الرَّحْمَنِ الرَّحِيمِ

Ramadan
Daily Planner

RAMADAN DAY: **DATE:**   **FASTING:** YES NO

IBADAH CHECKLIST

- ◯ Fasting
- ◯ Fajr
- ◯ Dhuhr
- ◯ Asr
- ◯ Maghrib
- ◯ Isha

- ◯ Tarawih
- ◯ Witr
- ◯ Dhuha
- ◯ Tahajud
- ◯ Rawatib
- ◯ Dhikr

GOOD DEEDS

- ◯ Dhikr
- ◯ Dua
- ◯ _______________

- ◯ Sadaqah
- ◯ Study

HADITH OF THE DAY

PRIORITIES

____
____
____
____

QURAN READING

Surah: ____________   Ayah: __________

Notes:

____
____
____
____

WATER

◊ ◊ ◊ ◊ ◊ ◊ ◊ ◊

WHAT I AM GRATEFUL FOR TODAY

DAILY CHECKLIST

- ◯ Morning Adhkar
- ◯ Evening Adhkar
- ◯ Deed Of The Day
- ◯ Adhkar Before Sleep

- ◯ Istighfar
- ◯ Shukr
- ◯ Dhikr
- ◯ Charity

Ibadah Creations

Ramadan
Daily Planner

RAMADAN DAY: **DATE:**   **FASTING:** ◐ YES ◑ NO

IBADAH CHECKLIST

- ◯ Fasting
- ◯ Fajr
- ◯ Dhuhr
- ◯ Asr
- ◯ Maghrib
- ◯ Isha

- ◯ Tarawih
- ◯ Witr
- ◯ Dhuha
- ◯ Tahajud
- ◯ Rawatib
- ◯ Dhikr

GOOD DEEDS

- ◯ Dhikr
- ◯ Dua
- ◯ __________

- ◯ Sadaqah
- ◯ Study

HADITH OF THE DAY

PRIORITIES

____
____
____
____

QURAN READING

Surah: _____________   Ayah: _______

Notes:

____
____
____
____

WATER

◌ ◌ ◌ ◌ ◌ ◌ ◌ ◌

WHAT I AM GRATEFUL FOR TODAY

DAILY CHECKLIST

- ◯ Morning Adhkar
- ◯ Evening Adhkar
- ◯ Deed Of The Day
- ◯ Adhkar Before Sleep

- ◯ Istighfar
- ◯ Shukr
- ◯ Dhikr
- ◯ Charity

Ramadan
Daily Planner

RAMADAN DAY: | **DATE:** | **FASTING:** ◐ YES ◐ NO

IBADAH CHECKLIST

- ⬤ Fasting
- ⬤ Fajr
- ⬤ Dhuhr
- ⬤ Asr
- ⬤ Maghrib
- ⬤ Isha

- ⬤ Tarawih
- ⬤ Witr
- ⬤ Dhuha
- ⬤ Tahajud
- ⬤ Rawatib
- ⬤ Dhikr

GOOD DEEDS

- ⬤ Dhikr
- ⬤ Dua
- ⬤ _______________

- ⬤ Sadaqah
- ⬤ Study

HADITH OF THE DAY

PRIORITIES

____
____
____
____

QURAN READING

Surah: _____________ Ayah: _____________

Notes:
____
____
____
____

WATER

WHAT I AM GRATEFUL FOR TODAY

DAILY CHECKLIST

- ◯ Morning Adhkar
- ◯ Evening Adhkar
- ◯ Deed Of The Day
- ◯ Adhkar Before Sleep

- ◯ Istighfar
- ◯ Shukr
- ◯ Dhikr
- ◯ Charity

Ramadan
Daily Planner

RAMADAN DAY:

DATE:

FASTING: YES NO

IBADAH CHECKLIST

- ◯ Fasting
- ◯ Fajr
- ◯ Dhuhr
- ◯ Asr
- ◯ Maghrib
- ◯ Isha

- ◯ Tarawih
- ◯ Witr
- ◯ Dhuha
- ◯ Tahajud
- ◯ Rawatib
- ◯ Dhikr

GOOD DEEDS

- ◯ Dhikr
- ◯ Dua
- ◯ _______________

- ◯ Sadaqah
- ◯ Study

HADITH OF THE DAY

PRIORITIES

____
____
____
____

QURAN READING

Surah: _____________ Ayah: _________

Notes:

____
____
____
____

WATER

◇ ◇ ◇ ◇ ◇ ◇ ◇ ◇

WHAT I AM GRATEFUL FOR TODAY

DAILY CHECKLIST

- ◯ Morning Adhkar
- ◯ Evening Adhkar
- ◯ Deed Of The Day
- ◯ Adhkar Before Sleep

- ◯ Istighfar
- ◯ Shukr
- ◯ Dhikr
- ◯ Charity

Ibadah Creations

بِسْمِ اللهِ الرَّحْمَنِ الرَّحِيمِ

Ramadan
Daily Planner

RAMADAN DAY:

DATE:

FASTING: YES NO

IBADAH CHECKLIST

- ◯ Fasting
- ◯ Fajr
- ◯ Dhuhr
- ◯ Asr
- ◯ Maghrib
- ◯ Isha

- ◯ Tarawih
- ◯ Witr
- ◯ Dhuha
- ◯ Tahajud
- ◯ Rawatib
- ◯ Dhikr

GOOD DEEDS

- ◯ Dhikr
- ◯ Dua
- ◯ _______________

- ◯ Sadaqah
- ◯ Study

HADITH OF THE DAY

PRIORITIES

____
____
____
____

QURAN READING

Surah: _____________ Ayah: _______

Notes:

____
____
____
____

WATER

DAILY CHECKLIST

- ◯ Morning Adhkar
- ◯ Evening Adhkar
- ◯ Deed Of The Day
- ◯ Adhkar Before Sleep

- ◯ Istighfar
- ◯ Shukr
- ◯ Dhikr
- ◯ Charity

WHAT I AM GRATEFUL FOR TODAY

Ramadan
Daily Planner

RAMADAN DAY:	DATE:	FASTING: ◗ YES ◖ NO

IBADAH CHECKLIST

- ◯ Fasting
- ◯ Fajr
- ◯ Dhuhr
- ◯ Asr
- ◯ Maghrib
- ◯ Isha

- ◯ Tarawih
- ◯ Witr
- ◯ Dhuha
- ◯ Tahajud
- ◯ Rawatib
- ◯ Dhikr

GOOD DEEDS

- ◯ Dhikr
- ◯ Dua
- ◯ _______________

- ◯ Sadaqah
- ◯ Study

HADITH OF THE DAY

PRIORITIES

____
____
____
____

QURAN READING

Surah: _____________   Ayah: _________

Notes:
____
____
____
____

WATER

◌ ◌ ◌ ◌ ◌ ◌ ◌ ◌

WHAT I AM GRATEFUL FOR TODAY

DAILY CHECKLIST

- ◯ Morning Adhkar
- ◯ Evening Adhkar
- ◯ Deed Of The Day
- ◯ Adhkar Before Sleep

- ◯ Istighfar
- ◯ Shukr
- ◯ Dhikr
- ◯ Charity

Ramadan
Daily Planner

RAMADAN DAY: DATE: FASTING: ◐ YES ◑ NO

IBADAH CHECKLIST

- ◯ Fasting
- ◯ Fajr
- ◯ Dhuhr
- ◯ Asr
- ◯ Maghrib
- ◯ Isha

- ◯ Tarawih
- ◯ Witr
- ◯ Dhuha
- ◯ Tahajud
- ◯ Rawatib
- ◯ Dhikr

GOOD DEEDS

- ◯ Dhikr
- ◯ Dua
- ◯ ___________________

- ◯ Sadaqah
- ◯ Study

HADITH OF THE DAY

PRIORITIES

____
____
____
____

QURAN READING

Surah: _____________   Ayah: ________

Notes:
____
____
____
____

WATER

◊ ◊ ◊ ◊ ◊ ◊ ◊ ◊

DAILY CHECKLIST

- ◯ Morning Adhkar
- ◯ Evening Adhkar
- ◯ Deed Of The Day
- ◯ Adhkar Before Sleep

- ◯ Istighfar
- ◯ Shukr
- ◯ Dhikr
- ◯ Charity

WHAT I AM GRATEFUL FOR TODAY

Ramadan
Daily Planner

RAMADAN DAY: ______ DATE: ______ FASTING: ◐ YES ◯ NO

IBADAH CHECKLIST

- ◯ Fasting
- ◯ Fajr
- ◯ Dhuhr
- ◯ Asr
- ◯ Maghrib
- ◯ Isha
- ◯ Tarawih
- ◯ Witr
- ◯ Dhuha
- ◯ Tahajud
- ◯ Rawatib
- ◯ Dhikr

GOOD DEEDS

- ◯ Dhikr
- ◯ Dua
- ◯ Sadaqah
- ◯ Study
- ◯ ______

HADITH OF THE DAY

PRIORITIES

____
____
____
____

QURAN READING

Surah: ______ Ayah: ______

Notes:
____
____
____
____

WATER

◌ ◌ ◌ ◌ ◌ ◌ ◌ ◌

WHAT I AM GRATEFUL FOR TODAY

DAILY CHECKLIST

- ◯ Morning Adhkar
- ◯ Evening Adhkar
- ◯ Deed Of The Day
- ◯ Adhkar Before Sleep
- ◯ Istighfar
- ◯ Shukr
- ◯ Dhikr
- ◯ Charity

بِسْمِ اللّٰهِ الرَّحْمٰنِ الرَّحِيمِ

Ramadan
Daily Planner

RAMADAN DAY:　　　**DATE:**　　　**FASTING:** ◑ YES　◑ NO

IBADAH CHECKLIST

○ Fasting　　○ Tarawih
○ Fajr　　　○ Witr
○ Dhuhr　　○ Dhuha
○ Asr　　　○ Tahajud
○ Maghrib　○ Rawatib
○ Isha　　　○ Dhikr

GOOD DEEDS

○ Dhikr　　　○ Sadaqah
○ Dua　　　　○ Study
○ ____________________

HADITH OF THE DAY

PRIORITIES

____
____
____
____

QURAN READING

Surah: ___________　Ayah: ______

Notes:
____
____
____
____

WATER

◌ ◌ ◌ ◌ ◌ ◌ ◌ ◌

WHAT I AM GRATEFUL FOR TODAY

DAILY CHECKLIST

○ Morning Adhkar　　　○ Istighfar
○ Evening Adhkar　　　○ Shukr
○ Deed Of The Day　　　○ Dhikr
○ Adhkar Before Sleep　○ Charity

Ibadah Creations

Ramadan
Daily Planner

RAMADAN DAY: ____________   DATE: ____________   FASTING: ◐ YES ◑ NO

IBADAH CHECKLIST

○ Fasting   ○ Tarawih
○ Fajr   ○ Witr
○ Dhuhr   ○ Dhuha
○ Asr   ○ Tahajud
○ Maghrib   ○ Rawatib
○ Isha   ○ Dhikr

GOOD DEEDS

○ Dhikr   ○ Sadaqah
○ Dua   ○ Study
○ _______________________

HADITH OF THE DAY

PRIORITIES

____
____
____
____

QURAN READING

Surah: ____________   Ayah: ____________

Notes:
____
____
____
____

WATER

◌ ◌ ◌ ◌ ◌ ◌ ◌ ◌

WHAT I AM GRATEFUL FOR TODAY

DAILY CHECKLIST

○ Morning Adhkar   ○ Istighfar
○ Evening Adhkar   ○ Shukr
○ Deed Of The Day   ○ Dhikr
○ Adhkar Before Sleep   ○ Charity

بِسْمِ اللهِ الرَّحْمَنِ الرَّحِيمِ

Ramadan
Daily Planner

RAMADAN DAY:

DATE:

FASTING: YES NO

IBADAH CHECKLIST

- Fasting
- Fajr
- Dhuhr
- Asr
- Maghrib
- Isha

- Tarawih
- Witr
- Dhuha
- Tahajud
- Rawatib
- Dhikr

GOOD DEEDS

- Dhikr
- Dua

- Sadaqah
- Study

HADITH OF THE DAY

PRIORITIES

QURAN READING

Surah: ______________   Ayah: ______________

Notes:

WATER

WHAT I AM GRATEFUL FOR TODAY

DAILY CHECKLIST

- Morning Adhkar
- Evening Adhkar
- Deed Of The Day
- Adhkar Before Sleep

- Istighfar
- Shukr
- Dhikr
- Charity

Ramadan
Daily Planner

RAMADAN DAY: | **DATE:** | **FASTING:** ◐ YES ◐ NO

IBADAH CHECKLIST

- ◯ Fasting
- ◯ Fajr
- ◯ Dhuhr
- ◯ Asr
- ◯ Maghrib
- ◯ Isha

- ◯ Tarawih
- ◯ Witr
- ◯ Dhuha
- ◯ Tahajud
- ◯ Rawatib
- ◯ Dhikr

GOOD DEEDS

- ◯ Dhikr
- ◯ Dua
- ◯ _______________

- ◯ Sadaqah
- ◯ Study

HADITH OF THE DAY

PRIORITIES

____
____
____
____

QURAN READING

Surah: _____________ Ayah: _______

Notes:
____
____
____
____

WATER

◌ ◌ ◌ ◌ ◌ ◌ ◌ ◌

WHAT I AM GRATEFUL FOR TODAY

DAILY CHECKLIST

- ◯ Morning Adhkar
- ◯ Evening Adhkar
- ◯ Deed Of The Day
- ◯ Adhkar Before Sleep

- ◯ Istighfar
- ◯ Shukr
- ◯ Dhikr
- ◯ Charity

RACE TOWARDS JANNAH

DO YOU KNOW THAT THE COMPANIONS OF THE PROPHET MUHAMMED صلى الله عليه وسلم USED TO COMPETE WITH EACH OTHER IN GOOD DEEDS?

HOW ABOUT YOU JOINING THE RACE TOO WITH EVERYONE THIS RAMADAN AND GETTING JANNAH (PARADISE) IN REWARD?

ALLAH SAYS.."SO FOR THIS (PARADISE) LET THE COMPETITORS COMPETE." (AL MUTAFFIFEEN, 83:26)

RAMADAN DUAS

رَبَّنَا آتِنَا فِي الدُّنْيَا حَسَنَةً وَفِي الآخِرَةِ حَسَنَةً وَقِنَا عَذَابَ النَّارِ

RABBANA AATINA FID-DUNYA HASANAH, WA FIL AAKHIRATI HASANAH, WA QINA 'AZAABAN-NAAR.

OUR LORD, GRANT US IN THE WORLD WHAT IS GOOD, AND IN THE HEREAFTER WHAT IS GOOD, AND PROTECT US FROM THE PUNISHMENT OF THE FIRE.

(2:201)

RAMADAN DUAS

رَبَّنَا لَا تُؤَاخِذْنَا إِن نَّسِينَا أَوْ أَخْطَأْنَا

RABBANAA LAA TU'AAKHIZNAA IN NASEENAA AW AKHTA'NAA.

OUR LORD! CONDEMN US NOT IF WE FORGET OR FALL INTO ERROR.(2:286)

RAMADAN DUAS

اَسْتَغْفِرُ اللهَ رَبِّىْ مِنْ كُلِّ ذَنْبٍ
وَّاَتُوْبُ اِلَيْهِ

ASTAGHFIRULLAHA RABBI MIN KULLI ZAMBIN-

WA ATOOBU ILAIHI

I ASK FORGIVENESS OF MY SINS FROM ALLAH WHO IS

MY LORD AND I TURN TOWARDS HIM.

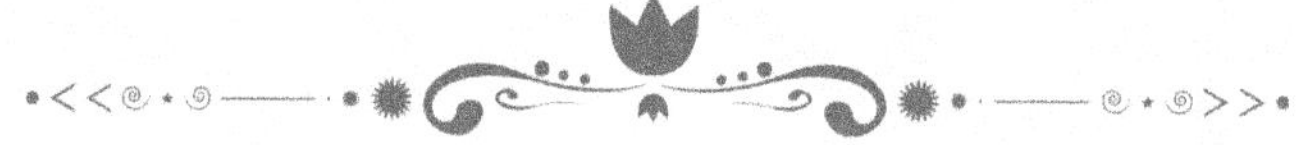

Laylat-al-Qadr - The Night of Power

Ramadan is a very special month in Islam, and its last ten nights are the most precious of all. Among them is a night so powerful and full of blessings that Allah has called it Laylat al-Qadr — the Night of Power.

This is the night when the Qur'an was first revealed, and worship on this single night is better than worship of a thousand months. On Laylat al-Qadr, angels descend to the earth with Allah's commands, and peace fills the night until dawn.

Allah says in the Qur'an:

"The Night of Decree is better than a thousand months.

The angels and the Rooh (Jibreel) descend therein by the permission of their Lord for every matter.

Peace it is until the emergence of dawn."

(Surah Al-Qadr 97:3–5)

"Indeed, We sent it (the Qur'an) down on a blessed night."

(Surah Ad-Dukhan 44:3)

Laylat al-Qadr- The Night of Decree

Laylat al-Qadr, the Night of Power, is the most special night in the Islamic calendar. It is the night when Angel Jibreel (Gabriel) first brought the verses of the Holy Qur'an to Prophet Muhammad ﷺ, beginning the guidance for all of humanity.

Many people believe it may fall on the 27th night of Ramadan, but the exact night is not known. That is why the Prophet ﷺ advised us to seek it during the last ten nights of Ramadan, especially on the odd-numbered nights, and to increase our worship just as he did.

Allah says in the Qur'an:

> "Seek Laylat al-Qadr in the last ten nights of Ramadan."

Allah has made this night better than a thousand months, which means that prayers, du'a, and good deeds done on this single night are rewarded more than those done over many years. It is a night filled with mercy, forgiveness, peace, and countless blessings.

DUA FOR LAYLAT-AL-QADR

DUA FOR LAYLAT-AL-QADR

HAZRAT A'ISHA (R.A.) SAID, "I SAID, 'MESSENGER OF ALLAH, IF I KNOW WHAT THE NIGHT THE NIGHT OF POWER IS, WHAT DO YOU THINK I SHOULD SAY DURING IT?' HE SAID, 'SAY:

اللّٰهُمَّ إِنَّكَ عَفُوٌّ تُحِبُّ الْعَفْوَ فَاعْفُ عَنِّي

> ALLAHUMMA INNAKA `AFUWWUN
> TUHIBBUL `AFWA FA`FU `ANNEE

"O ALLAH, YOU ARE PARDONING AND YOU LOVE PARDON, SO PARDON ME." (TIRMIDHI)

TABLE FOR PRAYER RAKAT

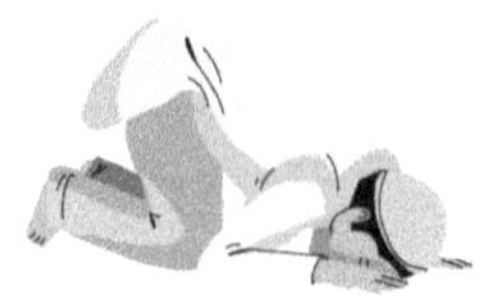

	SUNNAH	FARDH	SUNNAH	NAFL	WITR	NAFL	TOTAL RAKATS
FAJR	2	2	..	..	..	..	4
ZUHR	4	4	2	2			12
ASR	4	4	..	..	..	..	8
MAGHRIB	-	3	2	2	..	..	7
ISHA	4	4	2	2	3	2	17
JUMMAH	4	2	4+2	2	..	..	14

FARDH (FARZ) - THESE ARE MANDATORY OR OBLIGATORY PRAYERS. MISSING THESE ARE A SIN ON A BELIEVER

SUNNAH MUAKKADAH - THESE ARE MUSTAHABB (HIGHLY ENCOURAGED) AND THE PROPHET MUHAMMAD NEVER MISSED THEM.

WAJIB - THIS IS COMPULSORY BUT NOT THE SAME AS FARDH. MISSING IS A SIN BUT NOT THE SAME AS FARDH.

NAFL - THESE ARE OPTIONAL, PROPHET MUHAMMAD OCCASIONALLY PRAYED NAFL SALAH.

The Power of Sabr and Shukr

Allah reminds us that even in difficult moments, we should not give up or feel broken, because His help is always near. Hope keeps our hearts strong, and faith helps us move forward with courage.

True happiness does not come from having more, but from recognizing and appreciating what we already have. When we are grateful, our hearts feel lighter and our worries feel smaller.

That is why saying Alhamdulillah in every situation — in ease and in hardship — fills our life with peace, patience, and contentment. Gratitude turns what we have into enough, and hope turns our struggles into strength.

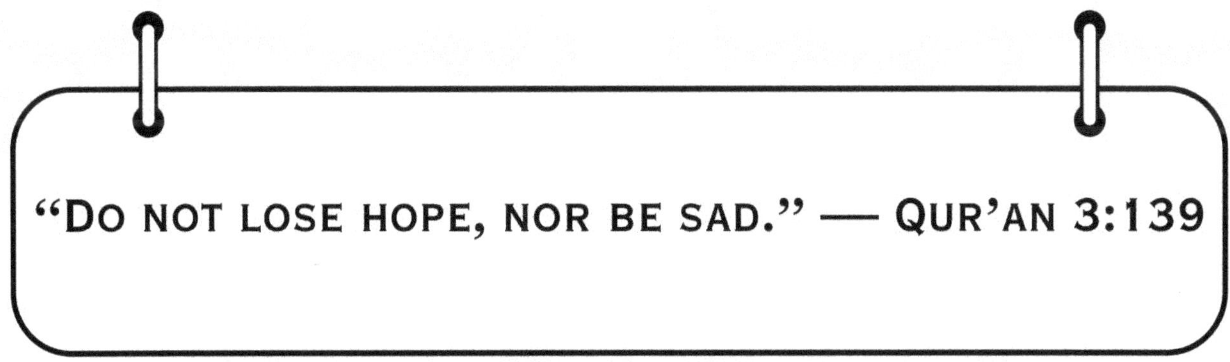

COLOR THIS EID CARD AND GIFT IT TO YOUR LOVED ONES

Alhamdulillah ! Its Eid

TAQABALLAHU MINNA WA MINKUM

May Allah accept (good deeds) from us and from you

IF YOU FOUND THIS PLANNER USEFUL, PLEASE POST A REVIEW ON THIS BOOK'S AMAZON PAGE. YOUR FEEDBACK IS VALUABLE FOR US AND WILL ENABLE US TO CREATE BETTER BOOKS.

IBADAH CREATIONS

Follow us on social Media:

Youtube : @ibadahcreations

Instagram: @ibadah_creations

Website: www.surahyaseen.info

Ibadah Creations

www.ingramcontent.com/pod-product-compliance
Lightning Source LLC
Chambersburg PA
CBHW040909130726
48005CB00019BA/3030